Notable Numbers

NATIONAL GEOGRAPHIC

Notable Numbers

0, 666 and other numerical beasts

Lamberto García del Cid

Our mathematical world

For Cristina, my love, my wife

© 2017, RBA Coleccionables, S.A.
© RBA Contenidos Editoriales y Audiovisuales, S.A.U.
Text by Lamberto García del Cid
English adaptation by Windmill Books and Vespa Design

Photographic credits: Aisa 31, 146; Album Akg 124; Album
    Lesing 140; Album Oronoz 25; RBA Archive 10, 11,
    12, 15, 18, 22, 28, 30, 32, 35, 46 left, 46 right, 48, 51,
    56, 60, 66 left, 66 right, 69, 72, 78 left, 80, 83, 92, 102,
    107, 123, 127, 129, 130, 137; Bill Gonyo 53; Buena Vista
    Television 71; Computer History Museum 78 right;
    Istockphoto 116; Honolulú Museum of Art 118; Library
    of Congress, Washington 153; Musée du Louvre 9; NASA
    151; Numberworld.org 41; Pirou 39; Rubin Museum
    of Art 120; Michael Stifel 145; Touchstone Pictures 70;
    University of California 108; The Yorck Project 19.

ISBN: 978-84-473-8927-8
Legal deposit: B9195-2017

Printed in Spain by RODESA, Villatuerta-NAVARRA

Contents

Preface

If you were to ask what the most notable numbers are on a computer, many people would answer 0 and 1, the two numbers of which its Universe is composed. However, they would be wrong, as there are peculiar numbers in any numbering system, such as palindromes or numbers that can only be divided by themselves and the unit (we call it 1), referred to as primes. In fact, there are many different types of numbers, a fertile numeric taxonomy that has shaped our tools of knowledge and, thus, our world view. We have natural numbers, integers, real numbers, rational numbers, irrational numbers, imaginary numbers, transcendental numbers, transfinite numbers, the list is literally endless. However, within these categories, taken as a whole or separately, not all numbers are of the same importance. There are numbers that are interesting and others that are not so interesting, depending on the point of view from which they are considered or the activity that makes use of them (or profits from them).

What makes a number important? There are numbers that are important to mathematicians, such as π; there are numbers that are important in certain religions, such as 3; and there are numbers that are important to lottery players, such as 22. The importance assigned to a number, be it arithmetical, mystical or superstitious, dates back to ancient times. For example, the symbol of Egyptian medicine was the eye of Horus, a god that was dissected by the evil Seth and cured by the benevolent Toth. Based on this myth, Egyptian doctors attributed mathematical values to the various sections of the eye of Horus — the tear duct had the value 1/2; the outer corner, 1/16; the iris, 1/4. This led to the proportions of medicines being expressed in relation to the so-called 'eye of Horus series', which allowed specialists to mix the various ingredients: saffron, lotus, ivy...

For the Greeks, the first ten numbers belonged to nature. They were spiritual entities, archetypes, symbols. If other numbers had a meaning, it came from combinations of these primitive numbers. This credo can be summarised by the phrase attributed to Pythagoras: "Everything is arranged according to the number." Plato, an adept Pythagorean, regarded the number as the essence of harmony, which in turn was the foundation of the Cosmos and humanity.

Throughout this book, we will consider representations of numbers in ancient times, a period, it must be kept in mind, in which the horizon for expressing an enormous number was set at the 'myriad', equivalent to 10^4, or 10,000, which was often used to designate large sets of elements, such as the members of an army.

However, for us today, a myriad represents just a small percentage of the spectators at a football match at a large stadium. The important numbers of antiquity were not always the same as those of modern times, and we shall spend time distinguishing one from the other. Modern maths did not just build on ancient concepts of numbers, but also invented new ones, numbers with names – and even surnames!

Although we have just noted that the ancients limited numbers to quantities that are small in comparison to those of today, this is not quite true. There is one exception found in the mathematics of India. The Indians were aficionados of enormous numbers, defining a cosmogony of near-arithmetical gods. This book also considers numbers from the Chinese civilisation, as well as numbers associated with good and bad luck.

Indeed, numbers, their importance and their influence, permeate the entirety of our everyday lives in a way that Pythagoras could scarcely have imagined, even in areas that appear far removed from them, such as poetry. This is why a contemporary poet such as Rafael Alberti does not hold back in his hymn to numbers, the poem *The Angel of Numbers*: "Virgins with set squares / and compasses, watching / the heavenly blackboards. / And the angel of numbers, / pensive, flying / from 1 to 2, from 2 to 3, from 3 to 4 [...] / Virgins without set squares, / without compasses, weeping. / And on the dead blackboards / the angel of numbers, / lifeless, wrapped in a shroud / on 1 and 2, / on 3, on 4."

To satisfy the curiosity of poets and readers alike, we shall try to show what lies behind, or in front of, the most notable numbers.

Chapter 1

Notable Numbers in Antiquity

Nomen omen – the name is a prophecy. This ancient saying could well be changed to 'the number is a prophecy'. From ancient times, the number has been used not only for prophecies but also to determine the fate of individuals and societies. The Assyrian–Babylonian religion structured the heavenly world around numeric harmony, a harmony governed by the Sumerian–Akkadian numbering system. The symbolism of numbers formed an inseparable part of the names of citizens and even the gods, who were also designated using cuneiform symbols. An example of this unique property can be seen in a tablet from the 7th century BC, which, together with the names of each god, contains a corresponding number: Anu, the god of the sky, is related to 60 (the major unit in the Sumerian–Babylonian sexagesimal system); Enlil, the god of the earth, is represented by the number 50; Ea, the god of water is assigned the number 40, and so on for the remaining gods.

In the Sumerian religion, each god has a rich symbolism and complex associations, including mystical numeric relationships. The illustration shows a Mesopotamian stele from the 12th century BC in which King Melishipak I takes his daughter to the goddess Nannaya and the triad of astral divinities. The Moon represents sin, the Sun is the god Samash and the morning star is Ishtar.

This peculiar use of numbers led the Neo-Pythagorean Moderatus of Gades, from the 1st century AD, to conclude that numbers were symbolic expressions of principles, in a similar way to how letters are symbolic expressions that combine to make words. Hence, numbers were symbolic representations of reality.

The importance of numbers was not just limited to the superstitious or supernatural. From the Greeks, numeric correspondences, their relationships and their consistency and rationalisation by means of systematic patterns, gave rise to calculation and the development of a discipline now known as mathematics. Indeed, it was the Greeks who distinguished between *logistike* (giving us the word 'logistics'), which comprised numbering and calculation, and *arithmetike*, which dealt with the theory of numbers. And it was arithmetic that Plato, a devout Pythagorean, insisted be taught to the citizens of his ideal republic. In this new field of knowledge, numbers had a utilitarian purpose (for calculation) that allowed them to free themselves from their symbolic value. However, it would take a while for the link to be severed, as the Pythagoreans, who were leaders in number theory, were precisely those who combined mathematical properties with mystical and symbolic ones.

A fragment of the Oxyrhynchus papyrus, which includes a fragment of Plato's Republic. *The Greek philosopher attached great importance to arithmetic and suggested its teaching should be obligatory.*

However, with or without the Pythagoreans, and in spite of them, the classical period has bequeathed us a profusion of notable numbers, numbers with symbolic meanings and properties that influenced the doctrines of the society of the time.

THE PYTHAGOREANS AND MATHEMATICS

In the 6th century BC, Pythagoras and his followers taught that everything was arranged according to numbers, albeit limited to the integers, and within these the natural numbers. Fractions were simply regarded as ratios of natural numbers. Therefore, the discovery that the square root of 2 ($\sqrt{2}$), the hypotenuse of the ideal square with sides of one unit, could not be expressed as a ratio of two natural numbers caused one of the greatest crises in mathematics.

According to the account of Anatolius, Bishop of Laodicea, around the year 280, the Pythagoreans were the first to use the name 'mathematics', which was regarded as '*the science*', something that is understandable if we consider that for them, mathematics was knowledge of numbers and geometric shapes, which they regarded as the essence of reality.

Print from the 19th century in honour of Pythagoras, philosopher and mathematician, about whose life little is known for certain.

Pythagoras and his followers described the relationship between the distance of a stretched string and the sound it made when plucked. They noted that shortening a given string to half of its original length produced a tone one octave lower than the first. From this came the notion that strings in the proportion 1:2 produce sounds that preserve harmony.

In terms of the theorem relating the three sides of a right-angled triangle ('the sum of the squares of the legs is equal to the square of the hypotenuse'), which is named after Pythagoras, it would appear this was taken from the Babylonians and Egyptians, who had already used it for solving problems. The Babylonians were also aware of 'Pythagorean triples', equalities of the form $x^2 + y^2 = z^2$ used for doubling squares. What really was discovered by the Pythagoreans was the triangular representation of the number 10, which they referred to as *tetraktys*. (This is discussed later.)

Regardless, the ideas of the Pythagoreans, the belief that the number permeated everything, that everything was based on numbers, has survived to the present day and continues to influence modern thought, both in the realm of science and beyond the limits of rationality.

PYTHAGOREAN MYSTICISM

Pythagorean thought, even if dominated by mathematics, also had a profoundly mystical aspect. The foundations of its doctrine included the idea of the immortality of the soul and transmigration – when someone died, their soul would pass to another body. There is no consensus as to whether Pythagoras himself taught in this field; however, many scholars believe that the famous Pythagorean idea of the transmigration of souls is too important to have been added by a subsequent follower. In his classic book *Lives and Opinions of Eminent Philosophers*, Diogenes Laertius (c. 200 BC) gives an account of Pythagorean cosmogony: "The principle of all things is the monad or unit; arising from this monad the undefined dyad, or 2, serves as the material substratum to the monad, which is cause; from the monad and the undefined dyad spring numbers; from numbers, points; from points, lines; from lines, plane figures; from plane figures, solid figures; from solid figures, sensible bodies, the elements of which are four, fire, water, earth and air; these elements interchange and turn into one another completely, and combine to produce a Universe animate, intelligent, spherical, with the Earth at its centre."

Pythagoreans Celebrate Sunrise, *an oil painting by Fyodor Bronnikov. The teachings of this school of philosophy entailed a curious combination of mathematics, music and mysticism, among other elements.*

Mythical numbers

This brief historical overview will not attempt to give a detailed analysis of the two most important numbers in antiquity – the golden ratio and the number pi – or deal with the fertile terrain of prime numbers. Instead, it will be limited to a description of the concepts and their importance.

The golden ratio (also known to the Greeks as the golden section and the divine proportion) is represented by the Greek letter Φ, pronounced 'phi', in honour of the sculptor Phidias, who appears to have used the number as an aesthetic proportion in his works. The number is a highly peculiar proportion that arises in a rectangle, giving it some unique properties, and which is known as the 'golden rectangle'. It is formed by a square and an extension, such that if B is the distance of the base of the original square and A is the distance of the base of the new rectangle that is formed, the following proportion holds: $A/B = \Phi = 1.6180339...$ This ratio or proportion is the Pythagorean golden number.

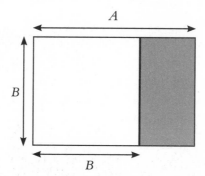

The unique property of this geometric figure lies in the fact that if we remove the square formed by $B \times B$, the sides of the resulting rectangle left behind (the shaded part of the drawing above) maintain the same proportion as the original shape. This property can only be found in golden rectangles. Such are the properties of the golden ratio, both arithmetic and aesthetic, that a great number of books have been written on it.

On the other hand, the number pi (π), which we can all remember from school, is – perhaps there is no harm in clarifying this – a fraction or decimal number that expresses the proportion between the length of a circumference and its diameter. Its value is $3.14159...$, although in school this is simplified to, at most, 3.1416. Numerous books and specific works have also been written on this number.

Finally, prime numbers are those that can only be divided by themselves and 1. This apparently simple property is responsible for certain unique characteristics that have made them some of the most intensely studied numbers. They also have another peculiarity that makes them unique: they exist in any numbering system, not just the decimal one. If our numbering system were base 36 or 12, it would also have prime numbers.

The first natural numbers and their importance

In antiquity, and here we are referring to the classical era of Greece, Rome, North Africa and the Middle East, the first natural numbers up to and including 10 were especially important. Let us consider them in more detail.

'Zero', that slippery concept

Before considering the natural numbers, it is useful to reflect a little on the concept of 'zero'. Various ancient civilisations, such as the Babylonians, Egyptians and Greeks, as well as the Mayans, produced mathematical or astronomical documents that show symbols used to indicate the value 0, although, for various reasons, it was not known how to put these to mathematical use. In ancient Egypt, for example, the Boulaq 18 Papyrus, dated to around 1700 BC, expresses the number 0 using the sign *nfr*. The Babylonians also tackled this subtle concept: in tablets dating back almost 2,500 years, a sign in the shape of a double nail, or double spike, with the meaning 'empty', appears. However, it does not appear to have been thought of in the sense of 'nothing' (the result of subtracting the same quantity, for example). That is why the author of a mathematical text from Susa expresses the result of subtracting 20 from 20 as "20 less 20… You see?"

In other entries, the commentary is more explicit: "The grain has been exhausted." However, this was not the only way in which the Babylonians designated this slippery concept. A tablet dated to around 700 BC, found in the ancient Mesopotamian city of Kish, uses a sign with three 'hooks'. In other tablets, just a single 'hook' is used, and in certain cases, it is bent into a shape similar to the current symbol for zero.

In his *Almagest*, written around the year 130 AD, Ptolemy often used the 'empty' symbol between digits or at the end of a number, although he did not use it as a number in its own right, only an element of notation. For their part, the Romans did not make any use of 'zero'.

On the other hand, 'zero' was being used in Mesoamerica long before appearing in Europe. As documented by a hieroglyph, the Mayans were using this concept as far back as the year 36 BC. However, it was in India where this value of nothingness was formalised in mathematical use; a great achievement that shall be considered in greater depth in chapter 4.

The Mayans had deep mathematical knowledge that included the use of 'zero'. The illustration shows a fragment of the Dresden Codex, related to astronomical matters and containing sophisticated calculations.

1

Curiously, the Greeks did not regard 1 as a number at all. They followed the teachings of Euclid, for whom a number is a composite of units, which 1 was not by definition. For them, 1 was the monad, the indivisible unit from which all other numbers arose. This was so because 1 came after emptiness, nothing – but not 0. The Greeks, like their neighbouring peoples, had not yet conceived of this concept. The Greeks realised that by adding 1 to an even number, it became odd and, vice versa, if it was added to an odd number it became even. This is why it became an arbitrator, a wild card.

The number 1 is present in the first numeric artefacts of humankind. Palaeolithic civilisations used unitary signs to establish their numeric series. It has been said that when humans discovered 1, they discovered themselves and the concept of individuality. In Islam, 1, the unit, is the symbol of the divinity, and is also identified with light. In the Hebrew alphabet, 1 is regarded as a male number and symbolises, together with the first letter, the *aleph*, the divine force. It is the separation of light from darkness; in the *Sefer Yetzirah* (The Book of Creation) it is said that all the words and all the shapes derive from the One Name.

A SIMPLE PATH TOWARDS 1

There are simple mathematical rules that allow us to return to the number one, the unit, or invisible monad, starting with any number. It is the only number that possesses this property. The process consists of taking any integer and applying three simple steps:

1. If the number is even, divide it by 2.
2. If the number is odd, multiply it by 3 and add 1.
3. Repeat the process until reaching 1.

Consider the number 17 as an example. As it is an odd number, we multiply it by 3 and add 1, giving 52. Dividing by 2 gives 26. Dividing by 2 again gives 13. As 13 is an odd number, multiply it by 3 and add 1, to give 40. Dividing by 2 gives 20, which gives 10 when divided by 2, which becomes 5 when divided by 2 again. As 5 is odd, we multiply by 3 and add 1 to give 16. As this number is even, we divide it by 2 to give 8, which when divided by 2 (the number is even) gives 4, which gives 2 when divided by 2, which, after a final division, gives the unit we require. It is possible to carry out this game with any other number and, even if the conjecture has not yet been fully proven, it will reach the unit. Try it for yourself.

The Greeks detected another unique quality in the number 1: it gives a greater result for addition than multiplication. In fact, it is the only natural number (today it is accepted as a number) with this peculiar property. Arithmetically, the number 1 has some unique properties: it is its own factorial, its own square, its own cube, and so on, for all powers. The number 1, as we know it today, originated in India, where it was represented using a horizontal, not vertical, line.

2

In antiquity, the number 2 had philosophical and theological importance, as it permitted duality, the conflict between two opposing principles: good and evil, even and odd, spirit and matter. In terms of religion, Manichaeism is perhaps the purest expression of this system, as it is based on a dualistic conception of the divinity and the Cosmos. However, in philosophy, the dyad —as 2 was known in Greece – also represents the principle of non-contradiction, in addition to the principle of the opposition between the self and the non-self, expressed in Chinese mysticism as yin and yang. Specifically, the number 2 is identified with the sign for yin, the feminine and the earthly.

For their part, the Pythagoreans regarded even numbers as feminine because they have the property of division through scissiparity (or bipartitioning). Odd numbers, on the other hand, were regarded as masculine. However, the Greeks were hesitant to accept 2 as a number, because, they argued, it has a start and an end, but no middle.

In esoteric symbology, the number 2 represents the echo, the reflection, and hence, conflict and comparison and the momentary immobility when two forces are equal. Geometrically, it is expressed by two dots, two lines or an angle; similarly, it represents the sexuation and mirror image of dualism. Two symbolises life and encompasses the two polar opposites: good and evil, life and death. This is why 2 is the number of Mother Nature, of *Magna Mater*, and many branches of esoteric thought regard it as potentially harmful.

In the Kabbalah, 'two' represents wisdom. However, for St Thomas, duality was a loathsome number. In numerology, 'two' corresponds to the mythological hero of the Sun, the god Apollo, who travels the firmament in a golden carriage.

From the mathematical point of view, and this feature was already known in antiquity, 2 is the only even prime number. That is why it holds a privileged place in the Olympus of numbers.

3

The number 3 was regarded as the symbol of perfect creation and divine unity. In fact, it is as if humans have an innate tendency to group concepts of the mind into three. For example, we repeat an experience or attempt a task three times before stopping. References to this ternary structure date back to the oldest records: three treasures, three voices, three warnings, three tests, etc.

For the Greeks, the number 3 was the first odd masculine number (the unit was regarded as more of a principle than a number). 3 is also the first triangular number. These triangular numbers, or their geometric images in the form of three joined points, provide the principle of formation and growth for all regular flat shapes and three-dimensional solids. The Greeks associated them all with the triangle, the simplest geometric shape with three sides and three angles.

On the other hand, 'three' is omnipresent in mythological accounts from history. There are three Furies in the levels of hell, three Moirai, three Graces, three times three muses and Paris had to choose between three goddesses.

The Three Graces, *a canvas by Raphael from 1504. Grouping things into*
threes has been a constant in human creation since the beginning of time.

In ancient Egypt, the gods, or other entities with divine properties, are grouped into triads. The main triads were: Theban Triad (Amun, Khonsu and Mut); the Abydos Triad (Osiris, Isis and Horus) and the Triad of Memphis (Ptah, Sekhmet and Nefertum).

In Greek and Hebrew numbers, *gamma* represents the number 3, and there is no mystic or religious school of thought in which that number does not express a concept of great importance. Specifically, many Hebrew practices and precepts are based on the number 3. In Genesis (18:1–19) we can find three angels that appeared to Abraham in human form. However, it is in the Talmud that we see the greatest proliferation of references to the number 3: "Our rabbis have taught that the saint, blessed may he be, weeps every day for three types of people: those who can study the Torah and do not; those who lack sufficient ability to study the Torah, but do so nonetheless; and for the government that governs the community with arrogance." The same book states that: "The saint, blessed may he be, praises three types of people every day: the single person living in a large city and who does not sin; the poor man who returns a lost object to its owner; and the rich man who pays his tithe without boasting." 'Three' is also present in assigning punishments and salvations: "All those who descend to hell will rise, except three who will descend but will not rise. These three are, he who commits adultery with a married woman; he who publicly shames his neighbour; and he who insults his neighbour." Continuing with eternal punishments in the Talmud, the school of Shammay teaches that on judgement day there will be three groups: "One for those who are fully upright; another for those who are fully perverse; and another for those who are neither one nor the other. The fully upright will be immediately inscribed and sealed for heaven. The fully perverse will be immediately inscribed and sealed for hell. Those who are neither one nor the other will descend to hell, howl, and then ascend."

For the Persian sect of Mazdek (its founder, Mazdek, born in Khorasan, was a social reformer who found an adherent in King Kavadh, and lived between 488 and 531), the Universe was made up of three elements: water, fire and earth. Their mixture gave rise to good and evil.

In Christian doctrine, 3 is a lucky number that has many meanings. Consider just a few examples of the triads that appeared in early Christianity: there are obviously three parts to the Holy Trinity (the Father, the Son and the Holy Ghost); the three major sins (greed, lust and pride); three forms of penitence (fasting, alms and prayer); those offended by sin (God, the sinner and their neighbour); the degrees of penitence (contrition, confession and atonement); the theological virtues (faith, hope and charity); the worldly dangers (*Tria Sunt pericula mundi: Equum currere, navigare et subtyranno vivere*) – three enemies of the soul (the devil, the world and the flesh) and three kings came to the infant Christ, while Peter later denied him three times. For St Augustine, the number 3 represented the soul and was in a certain sense an image of the divine.

Fragment of The Epiphany, *a triptych by Bosch painted between the end of the 15th century and the start of the 16th. The Christian religion is rich in all sorts of triads.*

In the Celtic world, triads and triples are continuously replicated. Questions are asked three times, gods are presented in threes and certain stone figures which represent diminutive beings with hoods (goblins and fairies we might call them now) that bring good luck always appear in groups of three. It was believed that the number 3 reinforces their power. 'Three' also figures in the legend of a quest imposed by the god Lugh on the three children of Tuirenn in compensation for the murder of their father Cian. They have to search for the three apples in the Garden of the Hesperides. Whoever eats them will not suffer hunger or thirst, or pain or illness. In addition, according to Celtic lore, three times the age of the dog gives the age of the horse; three times the age of the horse gives the age of the man; three times the age of man gives the age of the deer; three times the age of the deer gives the age of the eagle.

Another peculiarity of the Celtic culture, as noted by Julius Caesar, refers to the preference for oral forms over the written word when it comes to the transmission of knowledge. The druids preferred memory over writing. To aid them, they made use of sophisticated memory techniques, of which the triad was the most common, grouping things into threes. Laws, rules for poetry and traditional knowledge in general were thus organised in this way: "There are three things that are best done quickly: trapping a flea when you feel it; avoiding a rabid dog in your path; and smoothing conflicts" or "The three sources of wisdom: thought, intuition, learning".

It is possible that behind these triads, which appear in practically all civilisations, lies the schema of the family: father, mother and offspring. And perhaps also a way of thinking in cycles of three: beginning, middle and end; or thesis, antithesis and synthesis. The fact is that 3 is extraordinarily dynamic and rich in terms of its symbolism.

THE WRATH OF A KING AND THE THREE SECTIONS OF SCROLL

Azdaschir, king of Persia, had a secretary whose job it was to carry three sections of scroll when the sovereign met his subjects and sit beside the throne to observe his mood. If the king became angry, the secretary handed him the first section. In the event that the first reading did not have the desired effect and the king continued to be annoyed, the secretary handed him the second, and if he remained annoyed, he was handed the third. The first scroll read: "Calm yourself, since you are not a god, but flesh and bone, subject to confusion and to self-destruction." The second contained the following axiom: "Take pity on your subjects if you want god to take pity on you." And the third contained the following sentence: "Those who worship the one true god are entitled to the justice of a mortal."

4

For the Pythagoreans, the tetrad, or number 4, shared part of a feature of the dyad, of which it was the square, and was also the sacred aspect of the *tetraktys*, the fourth triangular number. The symbol also figured in the decad (10), as shown in the following figure.

For members of the Pythagorean brotherhood, the *tetraktys* diagram was an esoteric symbol, the significance of which equalled that of the pentagram. For the Pythagoreans, 4 and 8 were associated with harmony and justice, representing the first of the four elements: earth, air, fire and water. These were symbolised by the cube, the octahedron, the tetrahedron and the icosahedron. 4 is the principle feminine number and is identified with the geometric shape of the square, as it has four sides and four angles. For Greeks, numbers divisible by 4 were 'doubly even'.

Within the Christian tradition, the number 4 appears in the Old Testament: there are four rivers in paradise, one in each direction; this appears to have determined the decision that there were four gospels. For St Augustine, 'four' represented the body, in terms of its four qualities.

In the Talmud, it is said that the father has four obligations to his son – to circumcise him, to rescue him, to find him a wife and to teach him a trade. (There are some who also add: "and teach him to swim", although this fifth obligation can be discounted as it came at a later date.) In the Persian sect of Mazdek, God sat on his throne as a sovereign and there were four forces before him: discernment, intelligence, memory and happiness.

5

For the Pythagoreans, the number 5, or the pentad, was almost as important as the decad, as it was its half, its image reflected, or condensed. It is made up of the first odd, masculine number (3) and the first even feminine number (2), a property that meant it came to take on an erotic or amorous connotation for the Greeks. It became the number of love, or the number of Aphrodite, and hence it was also associated with marriage. The geometric emblem of 5 is the pentagram, a regular star with five points, which became a secret password and a geometric symbol of the Pythagorean brotherhood. The symbol appears to have already been known by the Babylonians, from whose heritage it was doubtlessly taken by the Greeks.

The human body represented inside a pentagram and surrounded by astronomical symbols, a drawing taken from the Third Book Concerning Occult Philosophy, *by Cornelius Agrippa. Since antiquity, the number 5 has had numerous esoteric connotations.*

The number 5 is the value of the hypotenuse of the Pythagorean (or right-angled) triangle, which is made up of sides with lengths 3, 4 and 5. The Pythagoreans also called the number 5 'natural', as when multiplied by itself, it gave a number that ended in 5. This property makes it the smallest of the 'automorphic' numbers. For his part, Plato recognised just five regular solids: the tetrahedron, the cube, the octahedron, the dodecahedron and the icosahedron; all of which, except the cube, are named according to their number of sides. The Torah, the Jewish law, is composed of the *Pentateuch*, or five sacred books, or the five books of Moses: *Genesis, Exodus, Leviticus, Numbers* and *Deuteronomy*.

The number 5 is also a lucky number in the Islamic religion and traditions, hence its proliferation in its teachings and precepts. There are five *takbir* for professing the Muslim faith, *Allah huwa akbar* ("God is greatest"); there are five prayers in the day; there are five days dedicated to Arafat; there are five fundamental elements of the pilgrimage to Mecca; there were five witnesses to the agreement of *Mubahala*, and there are five Koranic keys to the mystery (Koran, VI, 59; XXXI, 34). Other references to the number include Thursday, which has the Arabic name *al khiimis* (the fifth), regarded as a favourable day; the five sacred goods for the tithe; the five reasons for ablution; the five types of fasting; the pentagram of the five senses and marriage; the five generations that mark the end of tribal feuds; etc.

6

The number 6 was defined by Euclid as the perfect number as it is the sum of its factors ($6 = 1 + 2 + 3$). When considered alongside the fact that it is also the result of the multiplication of the same factors ($6 = 1 \cdot 2 \cdot 3$), this gives us an extremely peculiar number. For the Pythagoreans, the number 6 represents stability and equilibrium: it was represented by two equilateral triangles joined at their bases, a figure with six equal sides. They also associated it with marriage and the perfect union of the sexes: $6 = 3 \cdot 2$, where 3 is the first masculine number and 2 the first feminine number.

In the Talmud, the number 6 is often used to group characteristics or properties, such as in the following cases. "Human beings are characterised by six things: three relate them to the angels and the other three to animals. The three things relating them to the angels are, like the angels they have intelligence, they walk upright and talk in the sacred tongue. The three things that relate them to animals are that, like animals they eat and drink, breed and multiply, and defecate." "There are six things man enjoys the benefit of in this world, but whose capital is reserved for him for the next world. To provide accommodation to the traveller, to care for the sick, to have fervour in prayer, urgency to attend the house of studies, educating his children in the study of the law and judging his neighbour on his merits."

The importance of the number 6 in the Christian doctrine comes from St Augustine, who praises it as follows: "Six is a perfect number in its own right... God created the world in six days because six is a perfect number and it would remain perfect, even if his six days of labour had not existed." St Augustine also distinguishes between six degrees in the evolution of a person. In spite of the favourable opinion of this particular priest, certain sects of Christianity believe the number 6 corresponds to the devil, claiming that the snake tempted Eve on the sixth hour of the sixth day of creation.

For wizards and alchemists, 'six' represents organised nature, *natura naturata*, as it represents the number of faces of a cube.

7

The symbolic force of the number 7 lies in the idea of the triangle added to the square, or rather, the strength and robustness of the number 4 holding up the elegance and perfection of the number 3. This geometric coupling has the value of a complete cycle, the join between a primary state and a secondary one. This radiating force of the cycle is why there are seven days in the week and the stages of human life are sometimes divided into periods of seven years. Many other phenomena of a mystic nature were also measured in 7s. In the words of Hippocrates: "The number seven, on account of its hidden virtues, tends to be responsible for everything; it gives life and is the source of change, since even the Moon changes phase every seven days. The number influences all sublime beings."

This idea of giving rise to everything was taken up by Plato in the *Timaeus*, in which he describes the sequence of seven numbers that gave life to the Universe. The numbers were 1, 2, 3, 4, 8, 9 and 27, which were arranged in the shape of a lambda, as shown below.

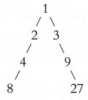

For the Pythagoreans, the number 7 was a symbol of virginity, due to the impossibility of dividing a circle into seven equal segments in a Euclidean construction, whereas this can be done using three and five segments.

The number 7 is the most sacred of numbers. Hence, it appears disguised in Chaldean and Hebrew mysticism. In the Bible, it is frequently cited in situations where magical or supernatural power is required, such as when God gives instructions to Joshua to take Jericho. He orders seven priests to carry seven trumpets in front of the arch on the seventh day, play them and walk seven times around the city walls. The magic power of the number took effect and the walls of Jericho collapsed.

The apostle St John introduced 'seven' in the Apocalypse. In his vision, there is a lamb with seven horns and seven eyes that receives a scroll containing the secrets of the destiny of man (there are seven of them). Upon undoing the first four seals, the four Horsemen of the Apocalypse appear. Upon undoing the fifth seal, the martyrs of the Roman persecution appear at the foot of the altar. When the sixth seal is broken, the day of wrath appears: the Sun turns black, the Moon becomes stained with blood, the stars of the sky fall to the Earth and mountains and islands move. When the lamb undoes the seventh seal, there is silence in heaven for half an hour. Then seven angels appear with trumpets and as they announce new disasters, hell fire and blood fall on the Earth.

The 'Whore of Babylon' riding the seven-headed beast, reproduced here in an anonymous German engraving, formed a central part of one of the passages of the Apocalypse. The number 7 plays a major role in this biblical book.

According to the ancient tradition of the Talmud, things have seven sides: six of these are determined by the two sides of each of the spatial dimensions, while the seventh is constituted by its inner aspect.

The number 7 also appears in the Jewish tradition in relation to the concept of *Shamayim*, or the multiplicity of heavens: seven heavens or palaces (*Heikhalot*) that mark the mystic root of the soul's ascent. The first heaven, or *Shamayim*, is the kingdom of wind and cloud, where Adam and Eve dwell; the second is *Raquia*, the kingdom of darkness, home to the fallen angels; the third is *Sagun*, which holds hell and paradise; the fourth is *Machonon*, the location of heavenly Jerusalem; the fifth is *Mathey*, the dwelling place of God, Aaron and the avenging angels; the sixth is *Zehbul*, the prison for fallen angels, a euphemism for demons; and the seventh and last, the most perfect, is *Araboth*, home to the throne of God.

THE SEVEN PALMS OF THE CANDELABRA

In his book the *Fable of Venice*, Hugo Pratt, an Italian graphic novelist of Sephardic descent, evokes the city's ghetto and an image of a mysterious hidden courtyard (Corte Sconta detta Arcana) reached by opening seven doors; once inside, the protagonist lights his way with a *menorah* or seven-branched candelabra. Every time one of the doors is opened, a candle goes out. The ghetto itself, deep inside, thus reproduces the structure of the symbol.

These seven palaces or seven castles, through which the soul must ascend, were later taken up by Western mystics, St Teresa (*The Seven Mansions*) and St John of the Cross, who, from a symbolic perspective explicitly based on the Apocalypse, states (verse 2, 4): "If, then, the soul conquers the devil upon the first step, it will pass to the second; and if upon the second likewise, it will pass to the third; and so onward, through all seven mansions, until putting the Husband in the wine cell which are the seven steps of love, until the Spouse shall bring it to the cellar of wine of His perfect charity." Scholem describes the same ascent in a similar way: "When I ascended to the first palace I was pious (*hassid*); in the second I was pure (*tahor*); in the third, just (*yashar*); in the fourth I was in union with God (*tanim*); in the fifth, I showed holiness before God; in the sixth, I read the *kedusha* before Him to ensure the guardian angels could do me no harm; in the seventh palace I rise with all my might and, while all my limbs tremble, I say the following prayer: Glory to You for you have exalted me, glory to You in the highest of mansions!"

In Islam, the number 7 enjoys similar prestige: there are seven heavens, seven earths, seven seas, seven levels of hell; pilgrims must walk round Mecca seven times. There are seven sacred nights and seven terrible days. Pilgrims must jump seven times over the fires of Anzara, in which seven different plants are burnt; they make seven genuflections over seven supports, and the *fatihal*, or opening chapter of the Koran, consists of seven verses.

The number 7 also appears as a symbol in Greek mythology: there were seven Hesperides, seven chiefs attacked Thebes (and the same number defended it) and there were seven sons and daughters of Niobe. Plato conceived of a celestial siren singing upon each sphere, and these 'seven sirens of the spheres' had to assimilate themselves into the seven fairies of legends and folk tales (one for each direction in space and time). According to certain authors, these theories correspond to the seven *lipíki* of Hindu esoteric beliefs (spirits related to each human plane: feeling, emotion, reflexive intelligence, intuition, spirituality, volition and divine foresight).

8

The Egyptians worshipped a group of four pairs of gods referred to as the *Smun* ('The Eight'), who personified the primitive forces of chaos: Nun and his wife Naunet symbolised the primitive water; Kuk and Kauket, the darkness; Hah and Hauhet, the eternity of space; and Amon and Amaunet, invisibility.

In the Talmud it is stated that, in remembrance of the command to light the candles at Hanukkah, it is necessary to light a lamp for each man and his home; a scrupulous person will light a lamp for each person in the house and an extremely scrupulous person will light eight lamps on the first day and gradually reduce the number by one a day. This is the teaching of the School of Shammay. However, the school of the Rabbi Hillel states that one lamp should be lit on the first day and the number increased by one a day until reaching 8. For the Greeks, arithmetically speaking, 8 was the second cubic number: 2^3.

9

For the Pythagoreans, 9 was the square of the first masculine number and the sum of two consecutive triangular numbers. For Hebrews, it was the symbol of truth, as it possessed the property that it reproduced itself through multiplication.

The number 9 plays an important role in Greek mythology. Think of the Muses, daughters of Zeus and Mnemosyne who protected the arts, sciences and letters. There are normally nine: Calliope, Clio, Melpomene, Thalia, Euterpe, Terpsichore, Erato, Polyhymnia and Urania. They were born on the summit of Piero and dwelt successively on the twin peaks of Mount Parnassus, in Phocis, Pindus, Thessaly, Helicon, Aonia and Boeotia, and rode the winged horse of Pegasus. Zeus frequently called them to Mount Olympus where they sung of the marvels of nature.

10

In antiquity, the decad was a model of perfection that reflected a divine order. For the Pythagoreans, 10 was the 'number of the world', as it brought together three qualities: it was double the pentad, representing the sum of two points contained in the *Tetraktys* and, as the decad, was the symbol of the Cosmos. It was the discovery of the musical intervals (the octave with ratio 2:1, the fifth with ratio 3:2 and the fourth with ratio 4:3) that led the Pythagoreans to regard the number 10 as sacred, as it was the sum of all the numbers formed by these primitive ratios: $1 + 2 + 3 + 4 = 10$.

For St Augustine, 10 was the number of justice and beatitude, the result of adding the Beast (represented by 7) to the Trinity (represented by 3). This is why, he argued, there are ten commandments from God. There are also ten elements of the *Sephirot* in the cosmology devised by Isaac Luria: "Before the creation there was only God. In order that there was something outside of him, he contracted his infinite Being and thus opened up spaces. This initial contraction of God is called *Tzimtzum*. In space, he created ten containers, or *Seriphot* to hold the emanation of the divine light. From this came the Universe, alongside everything that exists, including humanity."

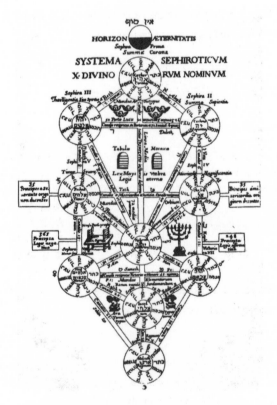

The number 10 is very significant in the Kabbalah. The illustration shows the Tree of Life with the ten Seriphot according to an engraving by Athanasius Kircher Oedipus Aegyptiacus (1652).

TRIANGULAR AND SQUARE NUMBERS

An ancient Greek custom was to represent numbers using sets of pebbles. There were different ways of grouping different numbers of pebbles. For example, the pebbles that represent the numbers 3, 6 and 10 could be arranged in triangles:

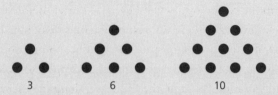

Such numbers were referred to as 'triangular numbers'. The Greeks also realised that if they calculated the consecutive sums of the natural numbers, in the order in which they are enumerated, the process would always give triangular numbers:

$$1 + 2 = 3.$$
$$1 + 2 + 3 = 6.$$
$$1 + 2 + 3 + 4 = 10.$$
$$1 + 2 + 3 + 4 + 5 = 15.$$
$$...$$

Continuing with the pebble notation, the Greeks discovered another regular shape into which they could group the stones: squares. For example, the numbers 4, 9 and 16 were expressed as follows:

These numbers were called 'square numbers'. The Greeks soon came to realise that square numbers were obtained by adding consecutive odd numbers.

$$1 = 1 \cdot 1 = 1^2.$$
$$1 + 3 = 4 = 2 \cdot 2 = 2^2.$$
$$1 + 3 + 5 = 9 = 3 \cdot 3 = 3^2.$$
$$1 + 3 + 5 + 7 = 16 = 4 \cdot 4 = 4^2.$$
$$...$$
$$1 + 3 + 5 + ... + (2n - 1) = n^2.$$

Other notable numbers from antiquity

In addition to the first natural numbers up to and including 10, which are of greatest importance in all symbolic and numeric systems throughout antiquity, there are other numbers that also form part of the magical and mystic imagination. We shall consider some of these below.

12

The number 12 has formed the basis of numeric systems, including the one used by the Sumerians of Mesopotamia, since around 3500 BC. The system, doubtless inspired by the lunar cycle, possessed (and still does) the advantage of being easy to divide. (It has a greater number of divisors than the base-10 system.) As a result of this system, we still count certain products by the dozen.

The number 12 has connotations of completeness (perhaps derived from this greater potential for divisibility) that has led to its appreciation among the creators of myths and religions. This is why there are 12 signs of the zodiac, the day is divided into 12 hours, there are 12 months in the year, 12 gods lived on Olympus, there were 12 Israeli tribes and there were 12 apostles.

Romulus instated 12 lictors (magistrates), and the Etruscan state was divided into 12 city-states. 12 is also the number of days specified by *Leviticus* for consecrating the

---

THE TWELVE LABOURS OF HERCULES

In Greek mythology, Hercules, or Heracles, was a god, the son of Zeus, who had to carry out 12 'labours' as punishment for atrocities committed in a fit of madness. The mythical hero had to overcome the following challenges:

1. The Nemean Lion. 2. The Lernaean Hydra. 3. The Erymanthian Boar. 4. The Ceryneian Hind. 5. The Stymphalian Birds. 6. The Augean Stables. 7. The Cretan Bull. 8. The Mares of Diomedes. 9. The Girdle of Hippolyta. 10. The Cattle of Geryon. 11. Cerberus. 12. The Apples of the Hesperides.

Hercules and the Hydra, *painting by Antonio Pollaiuolo.*

Detail from the atlas created in 1375 by Abraham and Jehuda Cresques, which shows a calendar with the 12 signs of the zodiac.

first tabernacle, in which 36 oxen, 144 rams and lambs and 72 male goats are offered, all of which are multiples of 12. The scheme of 12 is also used for the distribution of the winds on the compass rose (Eurus, Scolans, Notus, Auster, Africus, Euroauster, Zephirus, Stannus, Ireleus, Boreas, Aquilo, Volturnus). Similarly, there were 12 knights of the round table and 12 historical peerages in France.

15

In antiquity, 15 had erotic and sexual properties. In the cult of the Babylonian goddess of Ishtar, 15 was the sacred number obtained by multiplying five (an erotic number) and three (the genitals).

In Rome, 15 was chosen for appointing the priests responsible for the custody and consultation of the Sibylline Books, or the Sibyls. Hence they were referred to as the quindecemviri. Instituted by Tarquin the Proud, there were initially two (duunviri) and in the second half of the 4th century BC, the number was increased to ten (decenviri), until the Dictator Sulla added another five (quindecemviri).

19

The number 19 is extremely special to followers of Mohammed, as it is repeated throughout the Koran, either expressly, or hidden in instances of its multiples. Let us consider some of these references: the Koran contains 114 chapters, a multiple of 19; the famous invocation "In the name of Allah, the most compassionate, the most merciful" appears at the start of all chapters, with the exception of the ninth, but appears twice in the 27th chapter, or rather a total of 114 times; the first word (*ism*) appears 19 times throughout the text, the second (Allah) 2,698 times ($19 \cdot 142$), the third (*Al-Rahman*) 57 times ($19 \cdot 3$) and the fourth (*Al-Rahmin*) 114 times ($19 \cdot 6$). Finally, in chapter 74, hell is said to be guarded by 19 angels and the number is said to be an enigma to the unfaithful.

22

Sefer Yetzirah, or the *Book of Creation*, states that "22 letters are engraved by the voice, woven into the air and established by the mouth in five places. 22 letters he engraved, wove, weighed, changed, combined and created from them all possible forms, and all the forms that could be called into existence in the future." The text is referring to the 22 letters of the Hebrew alphabet; based on this usage, the number 22 takes on great symbolic importance. In fact, all alphabets of 22 letters are regarded as sacred because they are believed to reproduce the construction of the heavens and the manifestation of the divine word of humanity. There are also 22 cards in the major arcana of the tarot pack. In some ways, 22 means completeness.

Page from Diderot and D'Alembert's Encyclopaedia *on ancient and modern alphabets, which shows the 22 letters of the Hebrew alphabet.*

The Kabbalah is constituted by the study of the 22 letters of the Hebrew alphabet, which was and still is key to many adherents of the occult. It was soon discovered that there were many pertinent texts based on this number. St John describes his Apocalypse in 22 chapters. The *Ars Magna* by Ramon Llull consists of 22 chapters. Similarly, figures such as Eliphas Levi and Stanislas de Guaita deliberately split their teachings into 22 chapters.

26

The application of gematria (see box below) leads to the number 26, a divine number for Jews because of being the total of the values of the Hebrew letters that constitute the name of YHWH (Y + H + W + H = = 10 + 5 + 6 + 5 = 26).

It is an extremely special number for Sephardic Jews and corresponds to the number of knots tied in the four cords that hang from the edges of the corners of the prayer shawl. In this way, when they pray, Jews carry the numeric value of the name of God.

40

For ancient people, the number 4 did not only represent the square, but also the cube. It was used to indicate that something was complete, full, solid, strong, fixed, permanent and long-lasting. The symbolic force of the number 4 reaches its

---

GEMATRIA

Gematria is a numerological technique that involves assigning a value to the letters of the alphabet and looking for connections between words with the same value. The practice grew uncommonly quickly in ancient times and soon spread throughout the Mediterranean world, becoming a habitual pastime in learned circles. In the *Pseudo Callisthenes* it is said that the Egyptian god Serapis revealed his name to Alexander the Great in the following way: "Take two hundred and one, then one hundred and one, and then four times twenty and ten. Then put the first of these numbers at the end and then you will know which god I am." Arranging the words of the god underneath the letters gives:

Σ	Α	Ρ	Α	Π	Ι	Σ
200	1	100	1	80	10	200

---

maximum degree when multiplied by 10. Hence, 40 was the maximum multiplicity of the force of 4 or the completeness of 4, and everything that was 40 was the maximum degree of the idea of 4. Hence, Noah's Flood was the result of 40 days of rain, as 40 was already the degree of completeness, the highest sum.

50

The number 50 also has clear connotations of completeness, and appears with considerable frequency in Greek mythology: there are 50 danaides, argonauts, sons of Priam, etc. In biblical interpretations, the letter L = 50 represented the date of a jubilee:"Consecrate the fiftieth year" (*Leviticus*, 25:10), in addition to the repentance and forgiving of sinners, as people with five bad senses can comply strictly with the ten commandments ($5 \cdot 10 = 50 = L$). Let us not, as a curiosity, forget that for Roman men, it was a relief to indicate their age with an L , as whoever was able to do this was finally free from serving in the army.

100

The properties of the number 100 mainly derive from the 'roundness' conferred on it by the base of the decimal numbering system. In the scriptures, we read of the 100 years taken by Noah to build his ark, Abraham was 100 when he fathered Isaac, the 100 disputes, the 100 fasts of the Rabbi Zira, the 100 prophets hidden by Obadiah… 100 cubits for the measurement of Ezekiel's visionary temple, 100 sheep in *Matthew*, 18:12, etc. It is used for approximations that denote a 'large number', such as when someone asks:"What could a sheep do against 100 wolves?"

The hecatomb was a sacrifice of 100 oxen (*hekaton-bous*) offered by the Greeks in exceptional circumstances. One of these was the discovery of Pythagoras' theorem (let us not forget the number 100 is a Pythagorean number: $10^2 = 6^2 + 8^2$). In Greek mythology, the immortal Hydra had 100 heads. The Hydra was the offspring of Typhon and Echidna, killed by Hercules in his 11th labour to take possession of the golden apples in the Garden of the Hesperides.

153

The mystic properties attributed to the number 153 come from being the number of fish caught in the miraculous fishing trip on the Sea of Galilee (*John*, 12:11).

The number did not pass unnoticed by St Augustine, who carried out a complex numerological analysis to show there were 153 fish. The priest started from the number 10, the number of commandments and symbol of the ancient divine vision according to Mosaic Law, and added 7, the number of gifts of the symbol of the new vision, to give 17. He then added all the whole numbers from 1 to 17 to obtain 153.

THREE PLATONIC NUMBERS

Pythagoras exerted a clear influence on Plato. The idea that numbers permeate everything is present in many of his writings. Specifically, numerologists point to the presence of three numbers in his texts.

216: Plato alludes to this number (216, equal to 6^3) in an obscure passage from the *Republic*: "On it (216) can depend the best and worst generations in this imaginary republic." Like the Pythagoreans, Plato knew 6 was the first perfect number and that 216 represented the cube of this perfection.

729: The number has curious arithmetical properties: $729 = 3^6 = 9^3$. It is the second smallest cube that is the sum of three cubes: $9^3 = 1^3 + 6^3 + 8^3$. However, as $6^3 = 3^3 + 4^3 + 5^3$ (the sum of three cubes), 729 or 9^3 is also the sum of five cubes. This mysterious number also appears in the *Republic*: "Or if some person

Bust of Plato, conserved in the Vatican Museums in Rome.

begins at the other end and measures the interval by which the king is parted from the tyrant in truth or pleasure, he will find him, when the multiplication is complete, living 729 times more pleasantly, and the tyrant more painfully by this same interval."

5,040: is the factorial of 7 or $7! = 1 \cdot 2 \cdot 3 \cdot 4 \cdot 5 \cdot 6 \cdot 7$ and $5,040 = 7 \cdot 8 \cdot 9 \cdot 10$, which makes it a curious number because it is the product of consecutive natural numbers in two different ways. In *Laws*, Plato suggested that 5,040 was the number of men required for an ideal city, as it contained the largest number of consecutive subdivisions (59 divisors, as well as the number itself), meaning they could be easily divided up for reasons of peace or war.

The obvious symbolic sense of this number is given by the fact that $153 = 1{,}224 / 8$ (1,224 is the gematrian number for ιχθης ('fish') a symbol used by early Christians, and the number 8 repeated three times is associated with Jesus, Ιησους $= 888$).

365

One of the most prized goals of gematria has been to find the so-called God number. The Gnostics were among those who made the greatest efforts in this field. According to Basilides, the supreme leader of the Gnostics brought together the 365 secondary gods that presided over the days of the year. This is why the Gnostics describe God as "he whose number is 365". The magical power of the seven vowels, the seven notes of the scale, the seven planets, the seven metals (gold, silver, pewter, copper, iron, lead and mercury) are also involved. Whatever the name of the Indescribable was, Gnostics were sure it must involve the two magic numbers: 7 and 365. Based on this information, they resolved to find a name that combined both numbers and served as a pronounceable formula for the unutterable name of God. It was Basilides who succeeded in doing so with a name that lasted: *Abrasax* (or Abraxas), a name with seven letters and a numeric value of 365.

A	**B**	**P**	**A**	**Σ**	**A**	**Ξ**
1	2	100	1	200	1	60

$$\longrightarrow$$

365

10^{51}

This 52-digit number appears in Archimedes' *The Sand Reckoner*, which he dedicated to Gelo, King of Syracuse. In it, the mathematician describes his own system for counting extremely large numbers. He starts with the myriad, which represents the number 10,000, and which he defines as first-order numbers. He then describes a myriad of myriads, or 100,000,000 in our notation, which for Archimedes represented second-order numbers. He continued this cardinal ascent until reaching numbers of the order of many myriads of myriads. This allowed him to reach astronomical figures, numbers that in modern notation would be equivalent to $10^{80{,}000{,}000{,}000{,}000{,}000}$, an impressive number indeed.

888

The number 888 represents the gematria of the number of Jesus, as it is the number given by calculating the value of his name in Greek:

Jesus (ΙΗΣΟΥΣ)

Iota = I = 10
Eta = H = 8
Sigma = Σ = 200
Omicron = O = 70
Upsilon = Y = 400
Sigma = Σ = 200

Total = 888

After explaining his numeric orders, he then set to the task of counting, or trying to count, not only the number of grains of sand on a beach or in the whole world, but the number of grains of sand required to fill the entire Universe. To do so, he estimated that the head of a poppy contained no less than 10,000 grains of sand, and that its diameter is no less than 1/40 of the length of a finger, and assuming that the sphere of the fixed stars, which was the boundary of the Universe as far as Archimedes could tell, was less than 10^7 times the precise sphere that contained the orbit of the Sun in a large circle… The number of grains in the Universe was, in modern notation 10^{51}. (Compare this with the estimate by Edward Kasner and James Newman, that there are approximately 10^{20} grains of sand on Coney Island alone.)

Chapter 2

Notable Numbers in Modern Times

Having examined some of the notable numbers from antiquity, let us now consider more modern numbers. The chapter begins with a number, which like π appears everywhere, not just in mathematics but also in everyday life, infiltrating it in extremely subtle ways: it is Euler's number, or the number e.

The number e

After π, and similarly irrational and transcendental, the most famous number is the number e, defined as the limit of $(1 + 1/n)^n$ as n tends to infinity and whose value is 2.718281828... The number e was first studied by Euler, hence its name, although it is just a coincidence that the number bears the initial of this prestigious mathematician. In 1737, Euler himself proved that this number, before the same was proved of π, was irrational. In 1873, Charles Hermite (1822–1901) showed that e was also transcendental.

The French mathematician Charles Hermite (1822–1901) developed some of the properties of the number e.

The actual 'discovery' of this ubiquitous constant is attributed to the Swiss mathematician Jacob Bernoulli, who extracted it from a specific puzzle, referred to as the compound interest problem. However, it was recognised and used for the first time by the Scottish mathematician John Napier, who introduced the concept of logarithms into mathematical calculations. Hence, the number e is the base of natural or Napier logarithms (named after their discoverer).

The number e is regarded as the most important number in the field of calculus, principally due to the fact that the function e^x coincides with its derivative; as such, this exponential function often appears as the result of simple differential equations.

For his part, in 1665 Newton discovered that $e^x = 1 + x + x^2/2! + x^3/3! + ...$, which is the same as $e = 1 + 1 + 1/2! + 1/3! + 1/4! + ...$ Another characteristic of the number e is that like the number π, it is a transcendental number, meaning it cannot be directly obtained as the solution to an algebraic equation. As such, it is irrational and its exact value cannot be expressed as a finite number of decimal digits, or with periodic decimals. However, there are many attractive ways of defining e, such as:

$$e = 1 + 1/1 + 1/(1 \cdot 2) + 1/(1 \cdot 2 \cdot 3) + 1/(1 \cdot 2 \cdot 3 \cdot 4) + ...$$

Substituting the divisors for their short form, or rather for their factorial, the series is the same as the one we saw above, discovered by Newton, and letting $x = 1$:

$$e = 1 + 1/1! + 1/2! + 1/3! + 1/4! + ...$$

However, it is when expressed using continuous fractions, that it appears in the most harmonic and beautiful way:

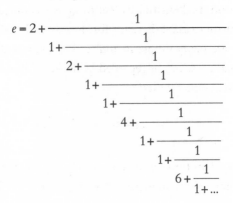

As a transcendental, curious and useful number, *e* has also had its admirers. In 1952, an electronic computer at the University of Illinois, under the supervision of D.J. Wheeler, calculated the number *e* to 60,000 decimal places. In 1961 Daniel Shanks and John W. Wrench Jr increased this number to 100,265 decimal places at the IBM data centre in New York. At present, the three largest records are held by Shigeru Kondo and Steve Pagliarulo, who calculated 200,000,000,000 decimal places of the transcendental number in May 2009; Alexander J. Yee, who calculated the number to 500,000,000,000 decimal places in February 2010; and Shigeru Kondo who teamed up with Alexander J. Yee to calculate 1,000,000,000,000 decimal places in July 2010.

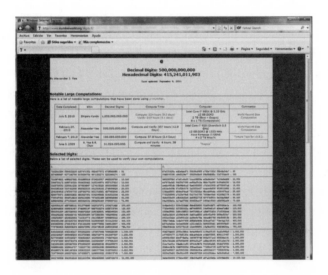

One of the many web pages dedicated to calculating the decimal places of numbers.
It contains all sorts of mathematical records.

The strange affection mathematicians feel towards *e* is similar to the way they feel about π, leading them to ask if there is a formula that relates both numbers. The answer is 'yes'. There are many simple formulae that connect them, but the best-known is Euler's equation, which is regarded as the most beautiful equation ever discovered, and represented as follows:

$$e^{i\pi} + 1 = 0; \text{ where } i = \sqrt{-1.}$$

Why do mathematicians find this equation so beautiful? The formula contains the most basic elements of mathematics. It contains the number 1, the start of the sequence of natural numbers. It contains addition, which can be used both to define the remainder of the natural numbers and the other three arithmetic operations: subtraction, multiplication and division. It contains 0, a concept that took millennia to be conceived by the human mind. It also contains the most important transcendental numbers: e and π. It contains the unit that defines the imaginary numbers: $\sqrt{-1}$, and, last but not least, by containing e, the equation is related to the infinite sequence $\lim_{n \to \infty}[1 + 1/n]^n$, which is another essential idea in mathematics.

A fable with interest

Let us now consider a practical example related to the number e. Like all the covetous minds of moneylenders throughout history, Taimish Monei never tired of asking

---

THE NUMBER e IN EVERYDAY LIFE

One could ask what the number e is used for or how it affects our everyday lives. π, as we all know, is useful for dealing with all sorts of circles and circumferences. Where there is a wheel or circular object, we can be sure the number π is buried therein. But e? Where is this peculiar number to be found? Let us consider some examples.

'War' is a card game in which two players share out all the cards: each player puts the first card from the ones they have been dealt on the table; the person with the highest card wins and if there is a draw they place their next cards on the table until one is greater than the other. If the game is played using two packs of cards, the probability of going through the whole pack without two cards of the same value being put down at the same time is exactly $1/e$.

The shape of the curve of the washing lines in some gardens (called a catenary) is defined by the following formula: $1/2 (e^x + e^{-x})$.

The limit of the returns from compound interest rates when the number of periods over which the interest is computed tends to infinity is e, expressed as $[1 + 1/n]^n = e$.

The population of animals and humans appears to grow in the same way as interest and is bounded by the number e. This type of growth is referred to as exponential growth; the inverse process is referred to as exponential reduction.

Applications of this unique number are also to be found in forensic medicine: it is known that the rate at which corpses lose heat is exponential, and e is used in the equation for determining how long an individual has been dead.

---

himself how he could increase his capital. Until then, the money he had lent had been governed by a simple interest rate, i.e.

$$I = P \cdot R,$$

where I, the interest, is equal to the principal (P), or original value loaned, multiplied by a rate (R), representing the interest.

It occurred to Taimish Monei that he could charge not just a percentage of the original loan, but also of the interest that was owed and had not been paid, giving rise to compound interest, calculated as follows:

$$A = P(1 + R/n)^n,$$

where A is the total amount owed to the moneylender from an original loan of P at an interest rate R and n is the number of times it is necessary to calculate the interest.

Taimish Monei lends 1,000 monetary units (m.u.) at an annual interest rate of 100%. At the end of the year, the poor debtor must repay 2,000 m.u.: 1,000 to return the principal and the other 1,000 as interest for the 'charitable' loan. To carry out the calculation, the first formula is applied, substituting P for 1,000 (m.u.) and R for 1.0 (100%), which gives 1,000 m.u. of interest.

After a number of years of obtaining 1,000 m.u., for each 1,000 loaned, Taimish Monei believes the time has come to increase the return on his 'generous' contribution to the progress of trade. Let us assume, however, that the law sets a maximum interest rate of 100% for loans. How could Taimish Monei overcome this barrier? He then has a brilliant idea. Why not lend money at 50% interest every half-year? This means he would lend the same amount of money plus, in the second half of the year, the interest earned during the first six months. And all of this without breaking the restrictions imposed by the law. Here the less than philanthropic moneylender realises that by applying the new way of lending money in two different periods, he obtains a greater return than before:

$$A = P(1 + R/n)^n,$$

where $P = 1,000$; $R = 1.00$ (or 100%), $n = 2$. Analysing the specific case gives:

$$A = 1,000\,(1 + 1.00/2)^2 = 1,000 \cdot (1 + 0.5)^2 = 1,000 \cdot (1.5)^2 = 2,250.$$

For 1,000 m.u. Monei obtains 2,250 m.u. at the end of the year. Is that not surprising? All without breaking the restrictions imposed by the law.

But Taimish Monei's greed knows no bounds. Always seeking to obtain more from his money, he asks himself: "What would happen if I upped the number of periods over which the interest is paid? Will my returns increase?" He decides to charge interest every three months, and establishes four annual periods with an interest rate of 25%. Hence, he continues to comply with the legal maximum of 100% per year. This new result gives:

$$A = 1,000 \ (1 + 1.00/4)^4 = 1,000 \cdot 1.25^4 = 2,440 \text{ m.u.}$$

Now the moneylender obtains almost 500 m.u. more than he did using simple interest. He appears to have struck gold. He then decides to increase the number of periods to 12 a year, calculating interest on a monthly basis:

$$A = 1,000 \ (1 + 1.00/12)^{12} = 1,000 \cdot (1.08333...)^{12} = 2,613 \text{ m.u.}$$

We can see that as Taimish Monei grows greedier, he establishes more periods over which the payment of the interest is calculated, earning more as a result of the loan. However, this leads to an inevitable question: does this increase have a limit, or is it possible to continue increasing it arbitrarily by simply increasing the number of periods over which the interest is calculated?

We can see where this leads by establishing daily periods for the calculation of interest, or rather 365 periods a year:

$$A = 1,000 \ (1 + 1.00/365)^{365} = 2,715 \text{ m.u.}$$

The increase over 2,613 m.u., obtained by using 12 periods in the year is not huge, but at least it is something. If we now calculate the periods for the compound interest in terms of hours, the result is 2,718 m.u. We can reduce the periods to minutes or seconds; however, it soon becomes clear there is a limit to which the result tends, in spite of the subdivisions. This limit can be expressed as follows:

$$\lim_{n \to \infty} [1 + 1/n]^n$$

The maximum return that can be obtained from 1 m.u., calculating the interest over an infinite number of periods, is the number $e = 2.71828182845...$

Negative numbers

A number (*n*) is said to be negative if it is neither 0 nor a positive number; the same as saying its value is less than 0. In modern notation, negative numbers are denoted by the prefix −, whereas the prefix for positive numbers is +. Hence, −3 is negative and +3 is positive. Sometimes we use +0 to emphasise that the 0 can be considered a positive number. However, it is incorrect to say −0, as there are no circumstances under which 0 is regarded as a negative number.

However, what does a negative number represent? Beyond the realm of pure mathematics, a negative number represents a quantity against, a lack, something that is not possessed or is owed. Negative numbers are used to measure values on a scale below 0, such as for temperatures, or to represent debts in financial transactions. In fact, the earliest merchants made use of the concept of debits and credits without being aware of the fact that they were subtracting negative numbers from positive ones. Their work was purely practical. The modern notation used to distinguish between positive and negative numbers (+ and −) also came about for commercial reasons, as these were the signs used by German merchants in the 15th century to note that a container was above or below an average weight. However, for mathematicians, the acceptance of negative numbers was not so simple.

The history of negative numbers in the West is the history of a lack of understanding. When Renaissance mathematicians came up against them, they were as suspicious as Diophantus had been or the Indian mathematician Bhaskara many years before. Hence, in spite of being aware of them, the majority of 16th and 17th century mathematicians did not accept them as true numbers or, if they did recognise them (always reluctantly), they did not accept them as solutions to equations. In the 15th century, Nicolás Chuquet, and in the 16th century, Michael Stifel, classified negative numbers as so-called absurd numbers. Only one person showed a deeper awareness of the rule of the signs: Gerolamo Cardano.

The French mathematician François Viète, a contemporary of Cardano, rejected negative numbers completely, whereas Descartes accepted them partially. Viète called the negative solutions of an equation false, arguing that they would need to represent numbers that were less than nothing. However, Descartes had shown that given one equation, it is possible to obtain another where solutions are larger than the original by a given quantity. Hence, using this method, an equation with negative solutions could be transformed into another with positive ones. As it was possible to change false solutions for others that were real, Descartes was willing to accept negative numbers. Pascal, however, regarded the act of subtracting 4 from 0 as completely meaningless.

Portraits of two great thinkers of the 17th century: Descartes (left) and Pascal (right).
The two men disagreed in a number of areas, including the issue of negative numbers,
upon which they held opposing opinions.

In fact, it was a friend of Pascal, the theologian and mathematician Antoine Arnauld, who would provide the most substantial argument against negative numbers of his day. Arnauld disputed whether $-1:1$ was equal to $1:-1$, arguing that -1 is less than $+1$; hence, how can a smaller number be to a larger like a larger to a smaller? The problem was widely debated among mathematicians of the time. In 1712, Leibniz agreed this was a valid objection, but argued that such proportions could be used for calculations because their form was correct.

One of the first mathematicians to accept negative numbers was Thomas Harriot, an English mathematician who died in 1621. In spite of not accepting negative roots, on one occasion, the mathematician made use of such a negative number in one of the terms of an equation. The Flemish mathematician Simon Stevin made use of positive and negative coefficients in equations, accepting negative roots in contrast to his English colleague.

In his book *Invention Nouvelle en l'Algèbre* (1629), the Frenchman Albert Girard regarded negative numbers on a par with positive ones, and provided the two solutions to a quadratic equation, even when both were negative. Somehow Girard realised that negative solutions go in the opposite direction to positive numbers, thus in a certain sense anticipating the idea of the numeric line. ("In geometry the negative indicates going backwards, whereas the positive indicates going forwards.")

In general, few mathematicians in the 16th and 17th centuries reached agreement or accepted negative numbers as such, barely recognising them as correct solutions to equations. They formed the basis of many curious beliefs. The English mathematician John Wallis, in his *Arithmetica Infinitorum* (1656), argued that as the ratio α:0, is infinite when α is positive, when the denominator is replaced with a negative number α:β with β negative, the ratio must be greater than infinity. A curious argument. Indeed, it was John Wallis who developed the exponential notation for negative powers based on just a few examples. Hence, he showed that if a series of inverses of cubes (1/1, 1/8, 1/27...), whose index is -3, is multiplied term by term with a series of squares (1, 4, 9...) whose index is 2, the result is the series (1/1, 4/8, 9/27...). The latter is 1/1, 1/2, 1/3..., a series of inverses of the first powers of the natural numbers whose index is $-1 = -3 + 2$.

Today, negative numbers are universally recognised and used in calculations just like positive ones. Their consolidation made it possible to discover a new type of number to which we shall now turn our attention: imaginary numbers.

Imaginary numbers

Almost as if the phrase 'once upon a time' should precede their study, imaginary numbers appear to lack real meaning. Leonhard Euler described them in the following way: "Neither nothing, not greater than nothing, nor less than nothing..." After regarding them as impossible because of their own nature, the

---

NEGATIVE NUMBERS FROM THE POINT OF VIEW OF ARITHMETIC

An algebraic definition of negative numbers states they can be regarded as an extension of the natural numbers, ensuring the equation $x - y = z$ has a solution z for all values of x and y. In terms of simple arithmetic operations, adding a negative number is the same as subtracting it from a positive one: $5 + (-3) = 5 - 3 = 2$ (in financial terms, if we have 5 m.u. and accrue a debt of 3 m.u., or spend them, we now have a net total of 2 m.u.). And subtracting a negative number is the same as adding its positive value: $5 - (-2) = 5 + 2 = 7$ (in financial terms, if we have 5 m.u. and repay a debt of 2 m.u., the new net value will be 7 m.u.). Multiplying two negative numbers gives a positive result. This can be better understood by regarding multiplication as the repeated addition of the same number: $-4 \cdot -3 = -(-4) - (-4) - (-4) = 4 + 4 + 4 = 12$.

famous mathematician suggested that as they already exist in the mind, there is nothing to prohibit their use in calculations. Leibniz was also surprised by this type of number, which he defined as "Almost an amphibian between being and not being." We can see that numbers that were so 'ethereal' and 'ghostly' were not liked by mathematicians.

It was Euler, in 1777, who christened the square root of the negative unit (-1) as i (for imaginary), in the pejorative sense of the word. All imaginary numbers can be written as ib, where b is a real number and i is the imaginary unit, with the property $i^2 = -1$. Imaginary numbers can be simple: $(a\sqrt{-1}) = ai$, or complex: $(a + b\sqrt{-1}) = a + bi$. Euler used $\sqrt{-1}$ in infinite series, leading him to discover his extraordinary formula $e^{i\pi} = -1$.

Curiously, after mathematicians revealed imaginary numbers, they came to be applied in a unusual ways, albeit 'appropriately', to the theory and practice of alternating currents. Hence, thanks to imaginary diagrams, it is possible to calculate, calibrate and control electrical transformers, equipment that is now fundamental to our everyday lives.

Leonhard Euler (1707–1783) made many contributions to mathematics. These include the first approximations to i numbers.

Finally, let us note that a curious property of these numbers is that when raised to different powers, they repeat a specific pattern (the sequence that is repeated is given in the box):

THE HISTORY OF IMAGINARY NUMBERS

The first negative square root known is $\sqrt{(81-144)}$, and appears in Heron of Alexandria's *Stereometrica*. Another, $\sqrt{(1{,}849-2{,}016)}$, was discovered by Diophantus as a possible solution to a second-degree equation. Neither mathematician took the matter seriously. If negative numbers were already regarded as false, absurd or fictitious in their own right, there is nothing unusual about their square roots being ignored. In the modern period, the first mathematician to write down a formula that included an apparently meaningless square root of a negative number was the Italian mathematician Gerolamo Cardano. Discussing the possibility of dividing the number 10 into two parts whose product would give 40, he showed that even though there is no rational solution to the problem, it is possible to obtain a solution using two impossible mathematical expressions: $5+\sqrt{-15}$ and $5-\sqrt{-15}$.

$$i^{-3} = i$$
$$i^{-2} = -1$$
$$i^{-1} = -i$$
$$\boxed{\begin{aligned} i^0 &= 1 \\ i^1 &= i \\ i^2 &= -1 \\ i^3 &= -i \end{aligned}}$$
$$i^4 = 1$$
$$i^5 = i$$
$$i^6 = -1$$
$$i^7 = -i.$$

Transfinite numbers

Infinity, that concept that is so difficult to grasp, represented by what looks to be a figure of eight on its side (∞), has caused no shortage of problems for mathematicians. As an algebraic operator, it was untameable, impossible to handle, but appeared every time a number was divided by 0. How could it be harnessed? For centuries, people preferred to ignore it completely, not taking it into account. This was because infinity was not regarded as a number but the representation of *all* numbers. Every time somebody carried out an operation such as $5/0 = \infty$, infinity would appear.

However, this was to change with the theories of one great mathematician: Georg Cantor. Born in St Petersburg in 1845, the son of German parents, Cantor had the idea that infinity could be used just like any other number and it was possible to work with it just like other numeric magnitudes. He also identified and proved the existence of various types of infinities, some larger than others. One infinity larger than another? Heresy. For Cantor, mathematicians' disdain for infinity and its nature – abstract and slippery – was due to an abuse of the concept, as the term *infinity* was applied indiscriminately to all non-finite sets. However, among these, it was possible to identify some that were, in a certain sense, measurable and of comparable sizes.

Cantor discovered the way to 'measure' the size of an infinite set and, in fact, to compare the size of two infinite sets to discover whether both were equal or if one was 'larger' than the other. He developed a rigorous theory with respect to these ideas: the theory of transfinite numbers. Taking the set of natural numbers, Cantor paired them with the set of even numbers and noted there were as many natural numbers as even numbers.

Even Numbers	Natural Numbers
2	1
4	2
6	3
8	4
10	5
12	6

For every whole number there is an even number that is its double. Hence, Cantor arrived at the surprising conclusion that with an infinity, the whole is not greater than its parts. For example, there are as many squares as there are numbers, as many cubes and as many numbers divisible by 10 or 1,000 as there are natural numbers. Through this research, Cantor realised there was no infinite set smaller than the set of natural numbers, and called this set aleph-0, or $\aleph_0$ (*aleph* is the first letter of the Hebrew alphabet). To distinguish this new type of numbers from finite numbers, he referred to them as 'transfinite'.

Georg Cantor with his wife in a photograph in 1880. This genuine mathematical genius developed the theory of transfinite numbers, thus taming a concept as tricky as infinity.

Cantor also realised that correspondence between natural and real numbers was impossible, unlike the previous correspondences shown, which led him to deduce that both infinities were not equal and that the set of real numbers, infinite in its own right, was greater than the set of natural numbers, which was also infinite. One infinity was, somewhat surprisingly, greater than another infinity. The first transfinite numbers that were introduced referred to the cardinality of certain sets and were represented using special symbols:

The cardinality of the real numbers: $card(\mathbb{R})$: c.
The cardinality of natural numbers, or aleph-0: $card(\mathbb{N})$: $\aleph_0$.
The cardinality immediately greater than a $\aleph_0$ is $\aleph_1$.

It is now possible to use the Zermelo–Fraenkel axioms to check that the three cardinalities above comply with $\aleph_0 < \aleph_1 \leq c$. The continuum hypothesis (on the cardinality of the set of real numbers) states that $c = \aleph_1$.

Some brief remarks on 0

The number 0 reached the West through the Arabs, who took it from India. It reached Europe through Andalusia, with the Muslim conquest of the Iberian Peninsula. The first manuscripts to show the use of 0s are the *Codex Vigilanus* and the *Codex*

Aemilianensis, both from the 10th century. Even if deciding who used the number 0 in Europe first is mired in controversy (there are those who claim it was in France by Pope Sylvester II around the year 1000), it is generally believed that the first person was the Italian mathematician Fibonacci (he of the famous sequence of numbers) in the 12th century, as it appears in his famous work *Liber Abaci* (*Book of the Abacus*). His use of it was extremely strange by modern standards, but at the same time so effective that Church authorities branded it as black magic and demonic, opposing its use until well into the 15th century.

In the West, the number 0 has had a large impact not just on mathematics, but also on esoteric symbolism. For certain schools of mystic thought, the number 0 represents the 'orphic egg', the non-being, and is mysteriously linked to the unit, which is its opposite and reflection. (In mathematics, any number raised to the power of 0 is equivalent to the unit.) 'Zero' symbolises death as the state into which the forces of the living are transformed.

However, 0's influence penetrates all areas of knowledge. For example, in 0, the philosopher María Zambrano sees the shadow of a whole that does not consent to be discerned, the emptiness of a fullness so compact that it is its equivalent. Poets also seem to be inspired by this nothingness in the form of a number. Caballero Bonald describes 0 in the following beautiful ways: "numeric surplus of nothing", "bordered pretext of absence", "magnitude that starts where it stops", "unborn and starting point", "silence that refers to another rule more neutral than silence…". And Antonio Porchia states that in his journey through the jungle of numbers that we call the world, he carried 0 as "a guide like a torch". Beautiful words for something so small. But is it small?

For American author Charles Seife, 0 is different from other numbers, as it makes it possible to view the indescribable and the infinite. This is why it has been feared, hated and even banned. Wormholes, concepts in physics that (theoretically) make it possible to move faster than light, come from a paradox originating as a 0 in Einstein's equation for general relativity. This is another proof of the importance of 0, according to Seife, who concludes in a rather apocalyptic manner: "Zero cannot be ignored. It does not only constitute the secret of our existence, but will also be responsible for the end of the Universe." Finally, the circular shape of 0 symbolises eternity: "On the Final Judgement day, the gates of heaven will be opened to the blessed. They will enter rolling, since they will have been reborn in the most perfect shape of all, the sphere. Thus has it been revealed by Origen." (A. Ireland)

THE POWER OF 0

For the mathematician and popular science writer Charles Seife, who has devoted an entire book to the number 0 (*Zero: The Biography of a Dangerous Idea*), this singular number is powerful because it is the twin of infinity, adding that a 0 or infinity underlies any revolution. To demonstrate the power of 0, Seife tells the following anecdote: "On 21 September 1997, off the coast of Virginia, the battleship *Yorktown* became stranded in open water. The *Yorktown* was designed to withstand the explosion of a torpedo or a mine, but nobody had conceived of a defence mechanism to protect it from 0. A grave error. A new program for controlling the engines had been installed on the computers of the *Yorktown*. Unfortunately, nobody detected the bomb represented by a 0 in the code, a 0 that should have been erased during installation. For one reason or another, the 0 was forgotten, hidden amongst the code. And there it remained, until required by the program, and causing the computer to crash. When the program tried to divide the boat's horsepower of 80,000 by 0, the engines were immediately paralysed. It took three hours to reset the emergency controls for the engine and bring the ship to the closest port. The engineers took days to extract the 0 from the program, repair the engines and leave the *Yorktown* ready for combat. No other number could have caused damage of similar proportions."

The battleship Yorktown, *which was immobilised in 1997 as a result of the 'simple' action of an out-of-place 0.*

Notable numbers from arithmetic

Let us now consider, without going into too much depth, a few numbers that are notable because of their arithmetical properties.

$\sqrt{2}$

The square root of 2, known as the Pythagorean constant, is a positive real number that gives 2 when multiplied by itself. Its numeric approximation is 1.41421356237309504880... It was possibly the first irrational number to be discovered. Legend has it that the Pythagorean Hippasus was thrown into the sea by his colleagues for having revealed this secret outside of the Pythagorean sect. Geometrically speaking, it is the length of the diagonal (hypotenuse) of a square with sides of length 1.

$\sqrt{5}$

The square root of 5 can be visually represented as follows:

$$\sqrt{5} = 2 + \cfrac{1}{4 + \cfrac{1}{4 + \cfrac{1}{4 + 1...}}}$$

2

The number 2 has many mathematical properties. It is the smallest prime number and the only even prime number. It is the first Sophie Germain prime number, the first prime factorial and the first Lucas prime. It is also an Einstein prime without an imaginary part and whose real part is of the form $3n - 1$. It is the third number in the Fibonacci sequence. Finally, 2 is the base of the simplest numbering system.

9

The number 9 is used in schools to check a division has been carried out correctly (the division by 9 test). Another curious property of this number is that if we take any number (of more than two digits) and subtract the sum of its digits, the resulting number is always divisible by 9. Try 8,754 as an example:

Adding its digits: $8 + 7 + 5 + 4 = 24$; $8,754 - 24 = 8,730$;
8,730 is a multiple of 9, as $8,730 / 9 = 970$, leaving no remainder.

17

The number 17 has an important property, as adding the digits of its cube gives the same number: $17^3 = 4,913$; $4 + 9 + 1 + 3 = 17$.

19

The number 19 is a prime number with certain curious properties: it is the sum of the first powers of 10 and 9, and the difference between the squares of 10 and 9. The first property needs no explanation, as they are the numbers themselves. However, the second does: $10^2 - 9^2 = 100 - 81 = 19$.

22

The number 22 is a palindrome, the square of which is also a palindrome: $22^2 = 484$.

37

This number has some curious properties. When multiplied by multiples of 3 it gives some strange results:

$$37 \cdot 3 = 111.$$
$$37 \cdot 6 = 222.$$
$$37 \cdot 9 = 333.$$
$$37 \cdot 12 = 444.$$
$$\ldots$$
$$37 \cdot 27 = 999.$$

The sum of its digits multiplied by itself is equal to the cubes of its digits. This jumble of words is better illustrated through an example: $(3 + 7) \cdot 37 = 3^3 + 7^3$. Another curious property is that the sum of the squares of its digits less the product of its digits is 37: $(3^2 + 7^2) - (3 \cdot 7) = 37$. Let us now consider a multiple of 37 with three digits, for example $37 \cdot 7 = 259$. Switching the order of the digits, such that the last digit becomes the first, gives us the number 925. Doing the same with this number gives us 592. Both numbers are divisible by 37 (another number that possesses this peculiar property is 185, as 518 and 851 are also multiples of 37).

69

The square of the number 69 (69^2) is 4,761, and its cube (69^3) is 328,509. The two results contain all the digits from 0 to 9.

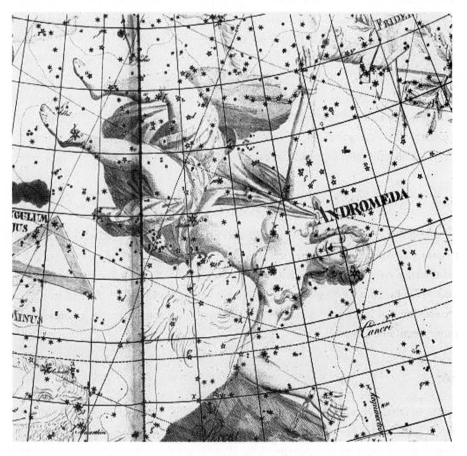

Illustration from Uranographia, *by Johann Elert Bode (1747–1826), the astronomer who gave his name to the sequence of numbers that facilitate the calculation of the distance between the planets and the Sun. The first seven numbers are: 4, 7, 10, 16, 28, 52 and 100.*

100

The number 100 is a composite number: $2^2 \cdot 5^2 = 10^2$. It is the result of adding together the first four terms in the sequence of natural numbers raised to the third power, along the lines of the cubic *tetraktys*: $100 = 1^3 + 2^3 + 3^3 + 4^3$. It is also the tenth square, and the seventh term in the Bode series, and represents the distance from Saturn to the Sun (in fact, the actual distance is 95.9 astronomical units).

199

The number 199 has various interesting properties: it is a prime number, it is an invertible prime number (if rotated 180°, it gives the prime number 661) and it is a permutable prime (199, 919 and 991 are all prime).

216

This number is the volume of the cube with sides of length $6 : 6^3 = 216$. It is also the smallest cube that is the sum of three consecutive cubes: $216 = 6^3 = 3^3 + 4^3 + 5^3$. And it is also the sum of two twin primes: $216 = 107 + 109$.

337

The number 337 is the largest permutable prime number, meaning that all the permutations of its digits give prime numbers: 337, 373 and 733. In our base-10 numbering system, the only permutable primes are: 2, 3, 5, 7, 13, 17, 37, 79, 113, 199 and 337. The number 11 is also a permutable prime. However, because all its digits are the same, it is referred to as the 'repunit' prime (a concept we shall consider in more detail in chapter 3).

365

One arithmetical property of the number 365 is the following: $365 = (10 \cdot 10) + (11 \cdot 11) + (12 \cdot 12)$; hence, it is equal to the sum of the squares of three consecutive numbers, starting with 10: $10^2 + 11^2 + 12^2 = 100 + 121 + 144 = 365$. However, it is also the sum of the squares of the two consecutive numbers 13 and 14: $13^2 + 14^2 = 169 + 196 = 365$.

648

This is the smallest number that can be expressed as ab^a in two different ways: $3 \cdot 6^3 = 2 \cdot 18^2$. This type of number is particularly rare. Here are some more:

$$648 = 3 \cdot 6^3 = 2 \cdot 18^2$$
$$2{,}048 = 8 \cdot 2^8 = 2 \cdot 32^2$$
$$4{,}608 = 9 \cdot 2^9 = 2 \cdot 48^2$$
$$5{,}184 = 4 \cdot 6^4 = 3 \cdot 12^3$$
$$41{,}472 = 3 \cdot 24^3 = 2 \cdot 144^2$$
$$52{,}488 = 8 \cdot 3^8 = 2 \cdot 162^2$$
$$472{,}392 = 3 \cdot 54^3 = 2 \cdot 486^2$$
$$500{,}000 = 5 \cdot 10^5 = 2 \cdot 500^2$$
$$524{,}288 = 8 \cdot 4^8 = 2 \cdot 512^2$$
$$2{,}654{,}208 = 3 \cdot 96^3 = 2 \cdot 1{,}152^2$$
$$3{,}125{,}000 = 8 \cdot 5^8 = 2 \cdot 1{,}250^2$$
$$4{,}718{,}592 = 18 \cdot 2^{18} = 2 \cdot 1{,}536^2$$
$$10{,}125{,}000 = 3 \cdot 150^3 = 2 \cdot 2{,}250^2$$
$$13{,}436{,}928 = 8 \cdot 6^8 = 2 \cdot 2{,}592^2$$
$$21{,}233{,}664 = 4 \cdot 48^4 = 3 \cdot 192^3$$
$$30{,}233{,}088 = 3 \cdot 216^3 = 2 \cdot 3{,}888^2$$
$$46{,}118{,}408 = 8 \cdot 7^8 = 2 \cdot 4{,}802^2 \ldots$$

729

This number is equal to 9^3 and is the second-smallest cube that is the sum of three cubes: $9^3 = 1^3 + 6^3 + 8^3$. However, as $6^3 = 3^3 + 4^3 + 5^3$ (the sum of three cubes), 729 or 9^3, it is also the sum of five cubes. Furthermore, $729 = 3^6$ and hence, it is 1,000,000 in base 3.

952

The number 952 is the peculiar product: $952 = 9^3 + 5^3 + 2^3 + 9 \cdot 5 \cdot 2$.

998

This number has a curious fraction: $1/998 = 0.001002004008016032064128256513$ $026052104208416833667334669\ldots$, a decimal in which the powers of 2 appear one after the other, until they begin to superimpose and break the pattern:

0.00**1**

0.00000**2**

0.00000000**4**

0.00000000000**8**

0.00000000000000**16**

0.000000000000000000**32**

0.0000000000000000000000**64**

0.0000000000000000000000000**128**

0.00000000000000000000000000000**256**

0.000000000000000000000000000000000**512**

0.0000000000000000000000000000000000000**1024**

0.00000000000000000000000000000000000000000**2048**

....

0.0010020040080160320641282565130260052...

1,001

One of the curious properties of 1,001 is that it is divisible by 7, 11 and 13, three consecutive prime numbers, the product of which also gives the aforementioned number. However, what is most interesting is not just that $1,001 = 7 \cdot 11 \cdot 13$ (there is nothing surprising here), but that multiplying a three-digit number by this number always gives a result in the form of the same number written twice, for example: $873 \cdot 1,001 = 873,873$, or $207 \cdot 1,001 = 207,207$.

This property is clear if we decompose the multiplication as follows: $873 \cdot 1,001 = 873 \cdot 1,000 + 873 = 873,000 + 873$.

1,089

Multiplying $1,089 \cdot 9$ gives 9,801, the same number but with its digits reversed. The property also holds for the numbers 10,989, 109,989, 1,099,989, and so on, adding 9s before the first 8. On the other hand, the fraction $1/1,089 = 0.000918273645546372819100091\ldots$ is periodical. Finally, if we reverse a three-digit number, subtract this reversed number from the first number and add the resulting number to the reverse of the resulting number, we always arrive at the number 1,089. Take 623 as an example: $623 - 326 = 297$ and $297 + 792 = 1,089$.

1,233

This number is curious because it is equal to $12^2 + 33^2$, or rather the sum of the squares of its first two and last two digits. Another example of a number with this property is $8,833 = 88^2 + 33^2$.

1,634

The curious thing about this number is that it is the sum of its components raised to the fourth power: $1^4 + 6^4 + 3^4 + 4^4$. The other four-digit numbers with this property are 8,208 and 9,474.

1,729

This number is famous thanks to an anecdote told by the English mathematician G.H. Hardy in his *A Mathematician's Apology*. On one occasion, Hardy visited his protégé, the Indian mathematician Ramanujan, in hospital. Making conversation, Hardy remarked that the number of the taxi that brought him there was 1,729, a very dull number, to which Ramanujan immediately replied: "No, Hardy! No! It is a very interesting number. It is the smallest number expressible as the sum of two cubes in two different ways" ($12^3 + 1^3$ and $10^3 + 9^3$).

Godfrey Harold Hardy (1877–1947), an English mathematician who reflected on the aesthetic beauty of mathematics and who, among other greater contributions, made the number 1,729 famous.

3,333

Taking the square of this number ($3,333^2$) gives 11,108,889, and separating the number and adding both halves of its digits together gives $1,110 + 8,889 = 9,999$. This property is also shared by the number 6,666, as $6,666^2$ gives 44,435,556 and its two halves, 4,443 and 5,556, add up to 9,999.

5,040

As mentioned previously, this number is the factorial of 7, or $7! = 1 \cdot 2 \cdot 3 \cdot 4 \cdot 5 \cdot 6 \cdot 7$. Similarly, it is equal to $7 \cdot 8 \cdot 9 \cdot 10$, meaning it has the curious property that it is the product of consecutive natural numbers in two different ways.

6,174

This number is the constant obtained using the so-called 'Kaprekar process' applied to four-digit numbers. The process consists of taking a four-digit number, ordering its digits in descending and ascending order, and subtracting the smaller number from the larger. The process is repeated with the result and will always reach the number 6,174. Consider an example with 3,871: $8,731 - 1,378 = 7,353$; $7,533 - 3,357 = 4,176$ and $7,641 - 1,467 = 6,174$. In this case only three steps are needed, and while others may need more, the process will always reach the Kaprekar constant. Of course, 6,174 is also a 'Harshad number', as it is divisible by the sum of its digits:

$$6,174 / (6 + 1 + 7 + 4) \Rightarrow 6,174 / 18 = 343.$$

10,101

The number 10,101 is the product of four prime numbers: $3 \cdot 7 \cdot 13 \cdot 37$. Any two-digit number multiplied by 10,101 will give this number repeated three times. For example: $73 \cdot 10,101 = 737,373$ and $21 \cdot 10,101 = 212,121$. The reason becomes clear if we write the multiplication as follows:

$$73 \cdot 10,101 = 73 \, (10,000 + 100 + 1) = 730,000 + 7,300 + 73.$$

1,234,567.87654321

This number, which counts up from 1 to 8, and then back down from the second decimal place, is the peculiar result of a unique multiplication: $1,111.1111 \cdot 1,111.1111$.

4,729,494

This number appears as a coefficient in the equation discovered by John Pell that allegedly solves the cattle problem set out by Archimedes in his book *The Sand Reckoner*, which roughly states: "If thou art diligent and wise, O stranger, compute the number of cattle of the Sun." It is followed by a series of ambiguous rules that can be summarised as follows: the Sun god has a herd made up of a certain number of white, black, dappled and yellow bulls, in addition to cows of the same colour. The number of white bulls is half and the third part of the black plus the yellow; the number of black bulls is equal to the fourth part plus the fifth part of the dappled and yellow; the number of dappled bulls is equal to the sixth part plus the seventh part of the white and the yellow; the number of white cows is equal to the third part plus a quarter of the black bulls and black cows; the number of black cows is equal to the fourth part plus the fifth part of the sum of dappled bulls and dappled cows; the number of dappled cows is equal to the fifth part plus the sixth part of the sum of the yellow bulls and the yellow cows; the number of yellow cows is equal to the sixth part plus the seventh part of the sum of all the white bulls and white cows; finally, the sum of the black and white bulls is a square number and the sum of the dappled and yellow bulls is a triangular number. After interpreting the problem, John Pell arrived at the following equation: $u^2 - 4,729,494v^2 = 1$.

24,678,050

Surprisingly, this eight-digit number is equal to the sum of the eighth powers of its digits.

$$2^8 + 4^8 + 6^8 + 7^8 + 8^8 + 0^8 + 5^8 + 0^8.$$

73,939,133

This is the largest prime number for which all initial segments of its decimal expansion are also prime: $7, 73, 739, 7,393\ldots$ These numbers are referred to as right truncatable primes.

410,256,793

This number is a deletable prime, which means if its digits are deleted in a certain order, each resulting number is also a prime number without needing to change the order of its digits. The process can be repeated until only one digit is left. Consider the following example:

$$410,256,793$$
$$41,256,793$$
$$4,125,673$$
$$415,673$$
$$45,673$$
$$4,567$$
$$467$$
$$67$$
$$7$$

It has been conjectured that there is an infinite number of such prime numbers.

65,359,477,124,183

The products of this number are nothing short of peculiar:

$$65,359,477,124,183 \cdot 17 = 1,111,111,111,111,111$$
$$65,359,477,124,183 \cdot 34 = 2,222,222,222,222,222$$
$$65,359,477,124,183 \cdot 51 = 3,333,333,333,333,333$$
$$65,359,477,124,183 \cdot 68 = 4,444,444,444,444,444$$
$$65,359,477,124,183 \cdot 85 = 5,555,555,555,555,555$$
$$65,359,477,124,183 \cdot 102 = 6,666,666,666,666,666$$
$$65,359,477,124,183 \cdot 119 = 7,777,777,777,777,777$$
$$65,359,477,124,183 \cdot 136 = 8,888,888,888,888,888$$
$$65,359,477,124,183 \cdot 153 = 9,999,999,999,999,999$$

A VERTIGINOUS NUMBER

The largest number that can be obtained from three digits is 9! to the power of 9! raised again to the power of 9!. Bearing in mind that $9! = 9 \cdot 8 \cdot 7 \cdot 6 \cdot 5 \cdot 4 \cdot 3 \cdot 2 \cdot 1$, just thinking about the number is enough to give us vertigo.

357,686,312,646,216,567,629,137

This is the largest left truncatable prime number. It is similar to the right truncatable number we saw previously, but this time the numbers are removed from the left-hand side of each new number. Consider the following simple example of a left truncatable prime number: 632,647, 32,647, 2,647, 647, 47 and 7. The process can be repeated for the number in the heading of this section.

3,608,528,850,368,400,786,036,725

This enormous 25-digit number is obviously divisible by 25. However, removing the first n digits also gives a number that is divisible by n. Trying an example, taking the first 6 digits (360,852), we get a number that is divisible by 6; if we take the first 10 digits (3,608,528,850), the number is divisible by 10.

450!

The humanbcomputer Horacio Uhler, calculated the value of 450! in 1950 without the help of computers. He discovered that it has exactly 1,001 digits, and thus referred to it as the "factorial of One Thousand and One Nights".

Numbers that still have symbolic meanings

In spite of scientific advances and the prevailing rationality in the West, certain numbers have retained their symbolic, mystical or superstitious power. We have already seen some of these in the previous chapter, but let us now consider the symbolic connotations of modern times. We shall exclude ominous numbers, those that are believed to bring bad luck, as these will be discussed in chapter 5.

3

We have already seen how the number 3 was regarded as the symbol of perfect creation and divine unity in classical time, as if there was an innate tendency in the human mind to group concepts into three. Indeed, this property of the number 3 has survived to the present. Today the number is also used to group ideas, concepts and rituals. There are those who blame Hegel for having revived the magic cult of the number 3 by using it in his triangular arguments. The cult was thought to have died out in the 18th century, when the method of philosophy dons at the Sorbonne was all but forgotten. Their idea was to place Aristotelian logic alongside Catholic theology, and build a trinity of thought, feeling and volition. This was also reflected in the three qualities espoused by St Thomas: *integritas* (unity, completeness), *consonantia* (consistence, *decorum*) and *claritas* (ability of the word to enlighten).

Subdivision into three categories continues to be used by almost all modern thinkers. Hence, for example, for Aldous Huxley there are three types of intelligence: human, animal and… military. For the philosopher Daniel Dennett the brains of animals have evolved in three phases: the behaviour of *Darwinian creatures* is genetically determined; *Skinnerian creatures* (named after the American behaviourist psychologist B.F. Skinner) display a wide range of behavioural patterns but deploy them randomly; and humans are *Popperian creatures* (named after the philosopher of science, Karl Popper). A Popperian creature behaves in the same way as a Skinnerian creature but only within its own head, as a series of mental stimulations.

An extreme example of the influence of the number 3 on the consequences of thought is provided by the futurist Velimir Jlebnikov, who developed an entire theory based on key historical events based on this number. The Russian writer and visionary studied the dates of successive historical events and discovered that they all followed patterns that could be related using the number 3.

Let us consider some examples. The date of the Battle of Mukden is 26 February 1905, which ended the Russian eastward advance, an advance that began with the conquest of Isker. That took place $3^{10} + 3^{10} = 2 \cdot 3^{10}$ days before the fall of Isker, which was three centuries before on 26 October 1581. The Battle of Ankara, which took place on 20 July 1402 and established a barrier to the Western advance of the Moguls, occurred 3^{10} days after the conquest of Kiev by the Tartars, which took place on 6 December 1240, the date that marked the beginning of the campaign towards the east. The Battle of Kulikovo, which took place on 26 August 1380, halting the advance of the hordes to the east, occurred $3^{11} + 3^{11} = 2 \cdot 3^{11}$ days after Rome was looted by Alaric on 24 August 410, reducing Rome to ashes. The conquest of Constantinople by the Turks in 1453 limited the advance of ancient Greece towards the east, but the fall of the Greek capital occurred $3^{11} \cdot 4$ days after 487 BC, when the Greeks conquered Persia in their eastward expansion. Jlebnikov recounts many more cases of important historical events determined by the number 3 and its powers.

Another curious case of the influence of the number can be seen in the novel *The Hive*, in which Camilo José Cela uses it as the basic structure of the book. At first glance, he appears to play with multiples of 3 to represent the cells of the hexagonal hives, which he wants to identify with the various narrative collages. Hence, the narration spans three days and six chapters, and involved 396 characters.

Portrait of Velimir Jlebnikov (1885–1922) and the cover of one of his books, Zangezi. *The writer was fascinated by numerology and devised the so-called 'tables of destiny' in his search for the mathematical laws he believed governed history, past and future.*

7

The number 7 and its magical power has persisted, often surreptitiously, in many modern literary and philosophical constructs. In antiquity, especially in the Hebrew tradition, we see how the seven heavens, or *heikhalot* represent the obligatory journey of an ascending soul.

Today, the number 7 also exerts an influence and appears in the work of many artists and thinkers. One significant example is from Ricard Lamote de Grignon, a musician who won the City of Barcelona Prize in 1951 for his work *Enigmes*, a piece written for a symphony orchestra, choir and narrator. The work is inspired by the Apocalypse and is structured around the number 7, which provides various symbolic meanings. As was fashionable at the time, the work of Lamote de Grigon was divided into seven parts and the title (*Enigmas*) has seven letters. At the start of each part, a small group of instruments states an interrogative theme, made up of seven sounds, which comes to form a soft chord, over which the narrator reads verses that are subsequently taken up by the orchestra. Curiously, the work has been performed seven times in the Catalan Palace of Music since its première.

There have been many who opposed these types of beliefs, dating back to a Lutheran minister, Caspar Neumann (1648–1715), who fought against the numeric superstition of the time. Specifically this was the belief that the human body was governed by a seven-year cycle of illness. According to this superstition, every seven years, a person reaches a critical period in their health and well-being. The ages of 49 ($7 \cdot 7$) and 63 ($9 \cdot 7$) are regarded as especially critical, and represent periods of great danger. Neumann based his rebuttal on records of parish statistics dating back over half a century. Thanks to his statistics, he was able to prove that mortality rates did not coincide with such a numeric belief.

12

Because of its properties of division, the number 12 is also often used to structure works of literature. Hence, in 1969 the French writer Georges Perec, who was part of the OuLiPo (Ouvroir de Littérature Potentielle), devised the following writing project. After choosing 12 places in Paris (streets, squares, arcades) where he had lived or that were of special significance to him, he was to write two descriptions of the places every month, one always written in the specific place, trying to be as neutral as possible. Pen in hand, he would try to describe as best he could the houses, the shops, the people he came across, the signs and anything else that attracted his attention. The other description was to be written in a different place and was to make use of his memory, evoking memories of the time spent in there. Once the descriptions were complete, the idea was to place them in an envelope and seal them with wax so he could not see them again. The envelope was also to contain small objects or mementos of the time spent in the places – metro tickets, cinema tickets, receipts from bars... Perec wanted to make descriptions every year, following an algorithm referred to as the 'order 12 orthogonal Latin bi-square'. The idea was to describe each place at different times of the year and not describe the same two places in the same month. The experiment was to last 12 years until all the places had been described 12 times. He planned to collect 288 texts, but his plan was cut short by his death in 1981. The experiment had three aims – experience the ageing of places there and then again, in his memory and in his own writing.

27

In an attempt to give a mysterious edge to their writing or create a narrative legend, certain authors seek out numbers that fit with their designs and make use of them by adjusting details to fit the number. A curious example is the number 27, famous today among literature lovers as the 'Shandy' number. In his *A Brief History of Portable Literature*, Enrique Vila-Matas reveals the existence of a semi-secret society named Shandy, allegedly founded in 1924 at the mouth of the River Niger and including figures such as Marcel Duchamp, Francis Scott Fitzgerald, Walter Benjamin, César Vallejo, Vicente Huidobro, Rita Malú, Valery Larbaud, Pola Negri... etc., with a total of 27 conspirators. One of the requirements for remaining in the society was that the literary output of the members be minimal, portable in the sense that it could be transported in a suitcase. The fact that it was composed of 27 people does not appear to be a coincidence: this was the 'Shandy' number par excellence. Appearances of this number in the life of the league of portable literature include the following: the member Stephan Zenith was 27 years old when the society's first party was held in Vienna; Rita Malú was locked up in a Somali asylum for 27 years. Picabia, a member of the society, married on 27 December. A painting by Paul Klee dedicated to the number 27 brought together, in the eyes of the society, the light and shadow of the 'Shandies'. This painting could be seen in the house of the Countess of Vensept, a woman with 27 grandchildren and who lived at number 27 on a street in Paris.

On the other hand, 27 has become a tragic number in the history of rock music. Janis Joplin, an extraordinary example of a fleeting and excessive life died from an overdose of heroin at the age of 27 in a Hollywood hotel room. Jimi Hendrix also died at the age of 27, also from an overdose. Jim Morrison, the singer and soul of the legendary group *The Doors* was found dead in the bath of his Paris apartment at the age of just 27.

The Effects of Trim's Eloquence.

Illustration from the novel Tristram Shandy, *by Laurence Sterne, to which the writer Enrique Vila-Matas paid homage to the 27-member society in his* A Brief History of Portable Literature.

28

In 1969, the American otolaryngologist (ear, nose and throat doctor) George Thommen, published a book called *Biorythms*, which immediately became a best-seller. The theories it contained were inspired by the curious ideas of the Berlinner Wilhelm Fliess, a friend of Sigmund Freud. Fliess, an enthusiast of numerology claimed the numbers 23 and 28 were present in the structure and organisation of the Universe. Developing the theory in his book, Thommen claimed that from the moment we are born, the human being is conditioned by three different rhythms: a physical rhythm, with cycles of 23 days; an emotional rhythm, with cycles of 28 days; and a third, intellectual rhythm, with cycles of 33 days. The theory of biorhythms is still widely believed, as can be seen from the number of books on the subject in any bookshop.

42

We bring up this strange number out of admiration of Douglas Adams, author of the incomparable and highly entertaining *Hitchhiker's Guide to the Galaxy*. In this saga, made up of five books, the number 42, hitherto poor and unknown, assumes a cosmic importance. The passage featuring this number discusses the answer provided by the most powerful computer in the Universe, Deep Thought, to the Ultimate Question of Life, the Universe and Everything:

"Okay", said the computer before going silent. The two men grow tense. The tension was unbearable.

"The truth is that you're not going to like it", observed Deep Thought.

"Tell us!"

"Okay", replied Deep Thought, "the answer to the Ultimate Question..."

"Yes...!"

"of Life, the Universe and Everything..." said Deep Thought.

"Yes...!"

"Is..." said Deep Thought before pausing.

"Yes...!"

"Is..."

"Yes...!!!"

"Forty-two", said Deep Thought with infinite patience and majesty.

A still from the film version of Hitchhiker's Guide to the Galaxy, in the scene in which the most powerful computer in the world, after seven and a half million years of meditation and before an expectant crowd, reveals its answer to the meaning of life and 'everything else'.

The number, which hitherto had been practically unknown, was not completely obscure, however. In his book *Life: A User Manual*, Georges Perec uses 42 elements in each of his chapters, extracted from a number of lists he had prepared and combined using 21 different Latin bi-squares. Each bi-square took elements (objects, numbers of people, cited authors, actions, etc.) from two different lists (i.e. $21 \cdot 2 = 42$).

108: THE NUMBER OF *LOST*

The numbers 4 8 15 16 23 42 make up the numeric sequence that appears on innumerable occasions in the television series *Lost*. The numbers first appeared in the episode *Numbers* from season one, corresponding to the winning lottery numbers that made Hurley, one of the main characters, a millionaire. Hurley learned of these numbers through Leonard, in a psychiatric hospital, who in turn had originally heard them on a radio broadcast when carrying out military service in the Pacific. As a result of the run of bad luck experienced by Hurley after winning the lottery, he comes to suspect the numbers are cursed. In the final episode of the first season, Hurley sees the numbers engraved on the hatch of a bunker. In the episode *Adrift*, from the second series, it was revealed that they were the code that had to be entered into the bunker computer every 108 minutes ($4 + 8 + 15 + 16 + 23 + 42 = 108$). Entering the numbers reset the timer; if the operator failed to enter the numbers and confirm them in time, the timer displayed a series of hieroglyphs; during this brief period of time it was still possible to enter the numbers, press 'run' and reset the timer to 108 minutes. The equipment in the bunker had to be replaced every 540 days ($108 \cdot 5$), meaning that each pair of operators had to enter the code some 7,200 times ($7,200 / 108 = 66.666$).

In a documentary called *The Lost Experience* it was revealed that the six numbers are the numeric values of the so-called Valenzetti equation, a mathematical formula designed to predict the end of the world (from which we also get the ominous number 666).

137

Do you believe cutting-edge science – the physics that studies elementary particles and uses large hadron colliders – is far removed from the mysterious influence of numbers? Of course not. In physics, the number 137 is the constant of fine structure; without doubt it is the most mysterious number in modern physics. Squaring the elementary load e and dividing the result by double the product of c (the speed of light), h (the Planck constant) and ε_0 (the vacuum permittivity), gives $1/137$, the reciprocal of the fine structure constant. There is an anecdote which states that the Nobel Laureate in physics, Wolfgang Pauli, after his death, asked God where he had got the mysterious number 137 from. God gave him a bundle of papers filled with mathematical formulae and replied: "Here's the explanation". Pauli studied the formulae, frowned, lifted his head and said: "*Das ist falsch.*" ("This is false.")

Photograph of Wolfgang Pauli taken around 1930. The Nobel Laureate in physics dedicated a considerable amount of intellectual effort to the number 1/137.

Another physicist, Sir Arthur Eddington, who was one of the first to understand Einstein's revolutionary theory of relativity, believed the number 137 possessed mystic qualities. He attributed it to the physical equivalent of the powers attributed by numerologists to 666.

1,024

This number is equal to 2^{10}, and forms the basis of the following story. Imagine that one day you are introduced to a man called Mr Devilson. In return for signing a small contract, you are offered all the luck you could ever wish for in life. As proof that his offer is genuine, before making the commitment he demonstrates it. He enters you into a coin-tossing tournament, in which you have to compete against ten opponents. Mr Devilson informs you that thanks to his intervention, you will win the ten tosses. Intrigued by his proposal, you accept. You take on the first opponent and win. You win the second too. And the third, the fourth and so on until the ninth toss; regardless of whether you call heads or tails, the coin, tossed by a neutral referee always lands on the side that makes you the winner. Only the last toss remains. The last throw. You can hardly believe your luck. Before the final toss, Mr Devilson reminds you that if you win, you must sign the parchment that he is holding out casually with a drop of your blood. You think for a while, and as someone who is well versed in mathematics, you reflect on the probability of correctly guessing heads or tails ten times in a row. You say: "winning the first toss was not hard, the probability of getting it right was 50%. Winning twice in a row was harder, since the probability was $50\% \cdot 50\%$, which is the same as $0.5 \cdot 0.5 = 0.25$, a one in four chance. Following this line of reasoning, the probability of correctly guessing the tossing of a coin ten times in a row is 0.00097656%, equivalent to a one in 1,024 chance."

After the initial scepticism has passed, you tell Mr Devilson that you accept and proceed to the final toss of the tournament. And win. The coin obeys your prediction. Convinced such an intricate possibility could only be the result of the supernatural intervention of your sponsor, you sign the contract he presents to you. The small cut on your finger hardly hurts at all as you think about all that you will be able to obtain with the gift you have just received. It goes without saying that you have not seen the 1,023 players who have lost; how each of these players has a sponsor with a goatee beard similar to that of your Mr Devilson, who disappears each time his protégé loses. Indeed, devils know a lot about mathematics: they know that if they say the same thing to 1,024 players, one of them (it didn't have to be you, although there will always be a 'you') will be the winner. Mathematics does not tell us who will win, just that there will be a winner. And devils know this. They know that only 1,024 unsuspecting people are needed to trap a soul, in this case yours. Don't trust luck and probabilities! Especially if a well-dressed gentlemen with educated manners... and a goatee beard... tries to entice you with them.

Conclusion with a view

There are numbers with arithmetic developments that endow them with an aesthetic aspect, an aesthetic that we could say they share with the beauty of numbers, that universe of symmetries and harmony. Consider some examples.

$$1 \cdot 8 + 1 = 9$$
$$12 \cdot 8 + 2 = 98$$
$$123 \cdot 8 + 3 = 987$$
$$1{,}234 \cdot 8 + 4 = 9{,}876$$
$$12{,}345 \cdot 8 + 5 = 98{,}765$$
$$123{,}456 \cdot 8 + 6 = 987{,}654$$
$$1{,}234{,}567 \cdot 8 + 7 = 9{,}876{,}543$$
$$12{,}345{,}678 \cdot 8 + 8 = 98{,}765{,}432$$
$$123{,}456{,}789 \cdot 8 + 9 = 987{,}654{,}321$$

$$1 \cdot 9 + 2 = 11$$
$$12 \cdot 9 + 3 = 111$$
$$123 \cdot 9 + 4 = 1{,}111$$
$$1{,}234 \cdot 9 + 5 = 11{,}111$$
$$12{,}345 \cdot 9 + 6 = 111{,}111$$
$$123{,}456 \cdot 9 + 7 = 1{,}111{,}111$$
$$1{,}234{,}567 \cdot 9 + 8 = 11{,}111{,}111$$
$$12{,}345{,}678 \cdot 9 + 9 = 111{,}111{,}111$$
$$123{,}456{,}789 \cdot 9 + 10 = 1{,}111{,}111{,}111$$

$$9 \cdot 9 + 7 = 88$$
$$98 \cdot 9 + 6 = 888$$
$$987 \cdot 9 + 5 = 8{,}888$$
$$9{,}876 \cdot 9 + 4 = 88{,}888$$
$$98{,}765 \cdot 9 + 3 = 888{,}888$$
$$987{,}654 \cdot 9 + 2 = 8{,}888{,}888$$
$$9{,}876{,}543 \cdot 9 + 1 = 88{,}888{,}888$$
$$98{,}765{,}432 \cdot 9 + 0 = 888{,}888{,}888$$

$1 \cdot 1 = 1$

$11 \cdot 11 = 121$

$111 \cdot 111 = 12,321$

$1,111 \cdot 1,111 = 1,234,321$

$11,111 \cdot 11,111 = 123,454,321$

$111,111 \cdot 111,111 = 12,345,654,321$

$1,111,111 \cdot 1,111,111 = 1,234,567,654,321$

$11,111,111 \cdot 11,111,111 = 123,456,787,654,321$

$111,111,111 \cdot 111,111,111 = 12,345,678,987,654,321$

We'll end the chapter with another visually appealing formation, this time prepared by hand and not the product of an algebraic series. Indeed, numbers can also be arranged, without loss of precision, in visually pleasing formations, such as this multiplication in the shape of a Christmas tree.

$$
\begin{array}{r}
777,777,777,777 \\
\times\ 777,777,777,777 \\
\hline
7 \\
777 \\
77,777 \\
7,777,777 \\
777,777,777 \\
77,777,777,777 \\
7,777,777,777,777 \\
777,777,777,777,777 \\
77,777,777,777,777,777 \\
7,777,777,777,777,777,777 \\
777,777,777,777,777,777,777 \\
77,777,777,777,777,777,777,777 \\
\hline
86,419,753,086,249,913,580,247 \\
\times\ 7 \\
\hline
604,938,271,603,728,395,061,729
\end{array}
$$

Chapter 3

Numbers with Names (Even Surnames)

The taxonomy of numbers has moved on from the proto-Pythagorean numbers (the golden ratio, pi) and functional numbers (even and odd numbers, positive numbers, etc.) to occupy the realm of numbers with invented names (happy, perfect, amicable, narcissistic) and then numbers named after their inventors or in some cases named more generously after a friend. Let us now forget about proto-Pythagorean and functional numbers and turn our attention to various numbers with names. First of all we shall consider numbers with invented names before moving on to those with forenames – and surnames.

Numbers with strange invented names

Perfect numbers

Perfection is not just an attribute of the sublime, the utopian or the divine, but also of certain numbers. By definition a perfect number is one that is equal to the sum of its divisors, excluding the number itself. They are called 'perfect' because in ancient days this property received a divine interpretation. For example, in his book *City of God*, St Augustine (354–430) claims God created the world in six days, and hence 6 is a perfect number ($6 = 3 + 2 + 1$), just like 28 ($28 = 1 + 2 + 4 + 7 + 14$), which is the number of days taken by the Moon to travel round the Earth.

In fact, 6 and 28 are the first two perfect numbers. The next two are 496 and 8,128. In both cases, the sum of the divisors is equal to the original number.

$$496 = 1 + 2 + 4 + 8 + 16 + 31 + 62 + 124 + 248.$$
$$8,128 = 1 + 2 + 4 + 8 + 16 + 32 + 64 + 127 + 254 + 508$$
$$+ \; 1,016 + 2,032 + 4,064.$$

> ## CURIOSITY
>
> Examining the first four perfect numbers in detail (6, 28, 496 and 8,128), it is possible to conjecture that the perfect number *n* has *n* digits. However this is not the case. The next perfect number is 33,550,336. We might then be led to think that the last digit alternates between 6 and 8, however this is not the case either as the next perfect number is 8,589,869,056. We may then change our conjecture to state that even perfect numbers end with a 6 or an 8. This is correct: the next perfect number is 137,438,691,328.

In search of perfect numbers in bloom

The first four perfect numbers can be found in Nichomachus of Gerasa's *Introduction to Arithmetic* (1st century); the fifth perfect number, 33,550,336 appears in a manuscript from the 15th century; the sixth, 8,589,869,056, and the seventh, 137,438,691,328, were discovered by Cataldi in 1588. The eighth is $2^{30}M_{31}$ (where M_{31} is 2,147,483,647, the 30th Mersenne prime number) discovered by Euler in 1750. Later on, using

To the left, a page from an edition of St Augustine's City of God, *published in 1470. The priest made reference to various perfect numbers. Above, the Cray-2 computer in a photograph taken at the Computer History Museum in Silicon Valley; in the 1990s, the machine made it possible to calculate new and enormous numbers.*

electronic calculators, it was possible to calculate more, the last of which, $2^{74,207,280}$ $(2^{74,207,281}-1)$, has 44,677,235 digits.

In 1992, a Cray-2 supercomputer was used to calculate the Mersenne prime: $2^{756,839}-1$. Based on this number, it was then easy to calculate the largest perfect number known to that date:

$$2^{756,838}(2^{756,839}-1).$$

The number has 455,663 digits and writing it out completely would fill a 180-page notebook. At present, the largest perfect number that has been discovered is:

$$2^{3,021,376}(2^{3,021,377}-1),$$

which was derived from the largest prime number known at the time: $2^{3,021,377}-1$, also a Mersenne prime. In fact, whenever a new Mersenne prime of the form 2^n-1 is discovered, it is possible to create a new perfect number by multiplying it by 2^{n-1}. Hence, the prime number $2^{3,021,377}-1$ allows us to derive the 37th perfect number $2^{3,021,376}(2^{3,021,377}-1)$.

Almost perfect numbers

The number 16 is almost perfect because its factors, excluding 16 itself, add up to its value minus 1: $1+2+4+8=15$. As we shall see further on, when we come to discuss abundant numbers, that all powers of 2 are almost perfect numbers. There are no known odd perfect numbers.

If the sum of the factors gives a number that is higher than the number in question, instead of one that is smaller, the number is referred to as quasi-perfect. It is known that a quasi-perfect number must be the square of an odd number, which is also an odd number, although it is not known if such numbers exist. What is known however, is that if they do exist, they must be greater than 10^{35}.

Multiperfect numbers

The French mathematician Marin Mersenne discovered that the factors of 120 added up to $2 \cdot 120 = 240$ and challenged his friend Descartes to discover numbers where the sum of their factors was a multiple of the original number. Considering it in more detail, we have: $120 = 2^3 \cdot 3 \cdot 5$, and its factors $1, 2, 3, 4, 5, 6, 8, 10, 12, 15, 20, 24, 30, 40$ and 60 add up to $240 = 2 \cdot 120$. If we include 120 among its own factors, the sum is $360 = 3 \cdot 120$, and hence the number is often referred to as tri-perfect. Only six tri-perfect numbers are known: 120; 672; 523,776; 459,818,240; 1,476,304,896; and 31,001,180,160. All of them are even, just like perfect numbers. If an odd tri-perfect number did exist, it would have to be greater than 10^{70} and would need at least 11 prime factors.

Hundreds of multiperfect numbers are known up to order 9 (nine times the original number). One of the smallest-order numbers within the order 8 was discovered by the human computer Alan L. Brown, and its factors are: $2 \cdot 3^{23} \cdot 5^9 \cdot$ $\cdot 7^{12} \cdot 11^3 \cdot 13^3 \cdot 17^2 \cdot 19^2 \cdot 23 \cdot 29^2 \cdot 31^2 \cdot 37 \cdot 41 \cdot 53 \cdot 61 \cdot 67^2 \cdot 71^2 \cdot 73 \cdot 83 \cdot$ $\cdot 89 \cdot 103 \cdot 127 \cdot 131 \cdot 149 \cdot 211 \cdot 307 \cdot 331 \cdot 463 \cdot 521 \cdot 683 \cdot 709 \cdot 1{,}279 \cdot 2{,}141 \cdot$ $\cdot 2{,}557 \cdot 5{,}113 \cdot 6{,}481 \cdot 10{,}429 \cdot 20{,}857 \cdot 110{,}563 \cdot 599{,}479 \cdot 16{,}148{,}168{,}401$.

Amicable numbers

From antiquity, two numbers have been regarded as an amicable pair if and only if each number is the sum of the divisors of the other number, excluding the number itself. The only amicable pair that appears in ancient texts on arithmetic is 220 and 284. Let us consider how these numbers meet the condition:

> Divisors of 220: 1, 2, 4, 5, 10, 11, 20, 22, 44, 55, 110 (add up to 284).
> Divisors of 284: 1, 2, 4, 71, 142 (add up to 220).

In the Bible, it is said that Jacob offered his brother 220 sheep when he was afraid he would kill him; for Jewish scholars, 220 is a magic number. Amicable numbers also appear frequently in Arabic writing. For example, Ibn Khaldun (1332–1406) in his *Introduction to History*, recognises their marvellous virtues for preparing talismans and horoscopes, and also discusses their magic properties.

Effigy of Ibn Khaldun on a Tunisian 10 dinar note. The learned 14th-century Andalusian made reference to amicable numbers, which had been extensively studied by Arab mathematicians.

The interest in amicable numbers was passed down to Europe and hence they were studied by authors from the 16th century, such as Chuquet, Etienne de la Roche, Cardano and Tartaglia. However, it was the French mathematician Pierre de Fermat (1601–1665) who was the first in the West to obtain a new amicable pair. Applying a rule that was used by the Arab mathematician Abu-l-Hasan Thabit ibn Qurra in 1636, Fermat discovered two new amicable numbers: 17,296 and 18,416 (although in fact it appears both numbers had been discovered centuries earlier by another Arab mathematician, Ibn al-Banna). When he published them, Fermat challenged Descartes to find another pair, a challenge that the latter accepted. Two years later, in 1638, he announced them in a letter to Mersenne: 9,363,584 and 9,437,056.

Euler, known as the 'master of all mathematicians', continued to study the matter and in 1747 provided a list of 30 amicable pairs, which he later extended to 60. However, in 1909 it was shown that one of the pairs was false, followed by another in 1914. However, these errors must not detract from the achievement of the great Swiss mathematician.

The second-smallest pair of friendly numbers (1,184 and 1,210) was discovered by Niccolò Paganini. He discovered them at the age of 16 in 1866, having previously been overlooked by Fermat, Descartes and even Euler himself. And the third-smallest pair (12,285 and 14,595), which had also been overlooked by the previous mathematicians, was discovered by B.H. Brown in 1939.

At present, with the possibilities provided by computing, the number of amicable numbers has increased considerably. More than 400 such numbers are now known. As a curiosity, it should be pointed out that the majority of amicable numbers are often divisible by 3, although this is not a general rule.

Betrothed or quasi-amicable numbers

The numbers 195 and 140 constitute the second pair of quasi-amicable numbers. They satisfy the following condition:

$$\sigma(140) = \sigma(195) = 140 + 195 + 1, \sigma(m) = \sigma(n) = m + n + 1,$$

where $\sigma(n)$, or the divisor function, is the sum of all the divisors of n, including the number itself. They are close to being amicable numbers, hence the name quasi-amicable, although they are sometimes also referred to as reduced amicable pairs.

81

The first pair of quasi-amicable numbers is $(48, 75)$, followed by the pairs: $(140, 195)$, $(1,050, 1,925)$, $(1,575, 1,648)$…

The expansion of the first pair is as follows:

$$\sigma(48) = 1 + 2 + 3 + 4 + 6 + 8 + 12 + 16 + 24 + 48 = 124,$$
$$\sigma(75) = 1 + 3 + 5 + 15 + 25 + 75 = 124,$$
$$\sigma(48) = \sigma(75) = 48 + 75 + 1 = 124.$$

Sociable numbers

Sociable numbers have the same properties as amicable numbers, although instead of being grouped in pairs, they form larger groups. The sum of the divisors of the first number gives the second; the sum of the divisors of the second gives the third, and so on. The sum of the divisors of the last gives the first number. For example, the numbers 12,496, 14,288, 15,472, 14,536 and 14,264 are sociable numbers because they comply with the conditions described above.

Happy numbers

If numbers can be prime, perfect, amicable and betrothed, what's to stop them being happy or unhappy? Let us define the following algorithm: take a positive integer expressed using the decimal numbering system, and add the squares of its two digits to give another positive integer. The operation of adding the squares is repeated with this new number until reaching 1, or a cycle that does not contain it. The numbers that give 1 at the end of the process are referred to as happy; the others, by exclusion, are unhappy.

The number 203 is happy, because $2^2 + 3^2 = 13; 1^2 + 3^2 = 10; 1^2 + 0^2 = 1$. The following numbers are also happy: 1, 7, 10, 13, 19, 23, 28, 31, 32, 44, 49, 68, 70, 79, 82, 86, 91, 94, 97 and 100.

The number 4 is unhappy, because it contains a loop (4, 16, 37, 58, 89, 145, 42, 20, 4...), which means it is impossible to reach 1.

Aspiring numbers

A number is said to be aspiring when the following conditions are met: the sequence formed by adding its proper divisors, then the divisors of the result of this summation, and then those of the next number, and so on, ends with a perfect number. For example, 25 is an aspiring number, as its proper divisors are 1 and 5, and $1 + 5 = 6$, which is a perfect number.

Fortunate numbers

Prime numbers can be obtained using the so-called Sieve of Eratosthenes: all the natural numbers are written in order and the multiples of 2 are removed, then the multiples of 3 and so on. The remaining numbers are prime. Fortunate numbers can be found in a similar way: after writing all the natural numbers in order, the even numbers are removed, leaving only the odd numbers: 1, 3, 5, 7, 9, 11, 13, 15, 17, 19... After 1, the next number is 3, and hence every third number should be removed from the sequence, giving a new series of the form: 1, 3, 7, 9, 13, 15, 19... The first remaining number is 7, and hence every seventh number should be removed from the previous sequence, and so on, following the same process of elimination. The result is a series that begins 1, 3, 7, 9, 13, 15, 21, 25, 31, 33, 37, 43, 49, 51...

Portrait of Eratosthenes, a Greek mathematician who lived between the 2nd and 1st centuries BC and gave his name to the sieve method that allows us to find the prime numbers.

These numbers, perhaps because of having survived a relentless decimation, are referred to as fortunate and are numbers that share many properties with prime numbers. This may lead us to suspect that the properties belong to prime numbers not because their only divisors are 1 and the number in question, but because they can be calculated using the Sieve of Eratosthenes. It is probable that the numbers of any sequence derived from a similar sieve will have similar properties.

Narcissistic numbers

Numbers also like to contemplate themselves in the waters of arithmetic harmony. In the decimal number system, a number is said to be narcissistic when it is equal to the sum of the powers of its digits, all raised to the number of these digits. The smallest example that is known is 153, equivalent to $1^3 + 5^3 + 3^3$, and is followed by $370 = 3^3 + 7^3 + 0^3$. An impressive narcissistic number is shown below: $4^{10} + 6^{10} + 7^{10} + 9^{10} + 3^{10} + 0^{10} + 7^{10} + 7^{10} + 7^{10} + 4^{10} = 4{,}679{,}307{,}774$.

Evil numbers

We have already seen how numbers possess properties that can only be attributed to humans, such as happiness, friendship, etc. However, evil is also contagious and for this reason there are evil numbers. An evil number is a natural number whose expression in base 2 (binary) contains an even number of 1s. For example, 12 and 15 are evil numbers, as $12 = 1100_2$ and $15 = 1111_2$. The reason for this aversion towards 1 is unknown, but this is how the numbers have been defined nevertheless. When they contain an odd number of 1s, they are referred to as odious.

Palindromes

Palindromes are numbers that are the same when read in both directions, such as 242. However, this number has not been chosen at random, but because it has a curious property: when we add the number to itself, it gives another palindrome $242 + 242 = 484$. This latter can also be expressed as a palindrome: 22^2.

The largest known palindrome was discovered by Harvey Dubner in 1991, and is given by the expression: $10^{11,310} + 4{,}661{,}664 \cdot 10^{5,652} + 1$. Using 0_{100} to abbreviate a hundred 0s in a row, the number is $10_{5,651}46616640_{5,651}1$.

A SIMPLE PROOF THAT THERE IS AN INFINITE NUMBER OF PALINDROMES

Take the palindrome 24,642. The number can be made into another larger palindrome by simply interspersing 0s between its digits: 204,060,402. In turn, this new palindrome can be made bigger by interspersing two new 0s in the places where there is now a single 0. And so on until ∞.

Congruent numbers

Two integers are said to be congruent modulo m if they give the same remainder when divided by m. For example, 9 and 5 are congruent modulo 4, as both numbers give remainder 1 when divided by 4. Other examples: 72 and 47 are congruent modulo 5 (remainder 2), and 19 and 12 are congruent modulo 7 (remainder 5).

Abundant numbers

The number 12 is the first abundant number because it is less than the sum of its factors, excluding itself: $1 + 2 + 3 + 4 + 6 = 16$. Another example is 24, with divisors 1, 2, 3, 4, 6, 8 and 12, the sum of which is 36. 36 is greater than 24, so 24 is abundant. And its abundance is $36 - 24 = 12$. There are only 21 abundant numbers below 100, in this order: 12, 18, 20, 24, 30, 36... All of them are even.

Another way of defining these numbers (sometimes also referred to as excessive) is to say that a number n is abundant if it complies with the condition $\sigma(n) > 2n$, where $\sigma(n)$ is the divisor function, or rather the sum of all the divisors of n, including n itself. By definition, the 'abundance' of the number is the value $\sigma(n) - 2n$.

Abundant numbers are essentially numbers with a sufficient quantity of different prime factors. All prime numbers and powers of prime numbers are 'deficient', which is the opposite of abundant. Another rule establishes that all multiples of an abundant number are also abundant numbers. Similarly, all divisors of deficient numbers are also deficient numbers.

Repunit numbers

These are numbers made up of just 1s: 1, 11, 111, 1111... They are represented as R_n, where n is the number of 1s contained by the number. The only known 'repunit' primes are R_2, R_{19}, R_{23}, R_{317} and $R_{1,031}$. If R_n is a prime number, n must also be a prime number. However, the converse is not true: if n is prime, this does not mean that R_n will be prime. Consider this curious representation of R_{38}:

$R_{38} = 11 \cdot 909{,}090{,}909{,}090{,}909{,}091 \cdot 1{,}111{,}111{,}111{,}111{,}111{,}111$.
This is rooted in $38 = 2 \cdot 19$, which also allows us to write it as follows:
$10{,}000{,}000{,}000{,}000{,}000{,}001 \cdot 1{,}111{,}111{,}111{,}111{,}111{,}111 = R_{38}$.

Obviously, 'repunit' numbers are a special kind of palindrome.

Primorial numbers

These are numbers of the form $p\# \pm 1$, where $p\#$ is the product of all the prime numbers less than or equal to p. Hence, $3\# + 1 = 2 \cdot 3 + 1 = 7$, meaning that the primorial $3\# + 1$ is a prime primorial. However, not all primorials are prime. For example, $13\# + 1 = (2 \cdot 3 \cdot 5 \cdot 7 \cdot 11 \cdot 13) + 1 = 30{,}031 = 59 \cdot 509$, which is not prime but is primorial.

The largest primorial number known in 1993 was $24{,}029\# + 1$, discovered by Chris Caldwell and with 10,387 digits. However, today the largest known primorial prime is $1{,}098{,}133\# - 1$, with 476,311 digits. It was discovered in 2012 by a group calling itself $p346$ (PrimeGrid project).

Pyramidal numbers

Stacking cannonballs in such a way that each layer forms a square, the number of balls contained in the successive piles is given by the series: 1, 5, 14, 30, 55, 91, 140...

The general formula for the nth term in this sequence is:

$$\frac{n(n+1)(2n+1)}{6}.$$

Other pyramidal numbers can be defined by imagining that the balls are stacked in layers that take the shape of a pentagon, hexagon, etc. However, it is impossible to stack them following regular patterns.

The formula for calculating the number of balls contained up to the nth layer of a 'pentagonal pyramid', for example, is: $1/2n^2(n+1)$.

Cyclic numbers

A natural number with n digits is referred to as cyclic when, if multiplied by any other natural number between 1 and n, the result is made up of the same numbers, but cyclically displaced. The most famous example is the number 142,857, which becomes 285,714 when multiplied by 2, and 428,571 when multiplied by 3. A summary of its products up to the number 6 is given below:

$$142{,}857 \cdot 1 = 142{,}857$$
$$142{,}857 \cdot 2 = 285{,}714$$
$$142{,}857 \cdot 3 = 428{,}571$$
$$142{,}857 \cdot 4 = 571{,}428$$
$$142{,}857 \cdot 5 = 714{,}285$$
$$142{,}857 \cdot 6 = 857{,}142.$$

Another curious aspect of this type of number is that the sum of the first three digits and the last three digits, taken both in their normal and reverse order, adds up to 999,999. Is this because $142{,}857 \cdot 7$ gives 999,999?

We also have $142{,}857 \cdot 361 = 51{,}571{,}377$; adding this result by sections: $51 + 571 + 377 = 999$; or rather, $51 + 57 + 13 + 77 = 198$, which, adding its halves $(01 + 98)$, gives 99.

Rectangular numbers

Rectangular numbers are those that can be arranged in the form of a rectangle with one side greater than the other. This is easier to understand with an example. Consider the number 12, which is a rectangular number. There are two different ways of arranging this number in rectangles:

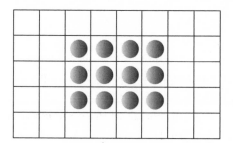 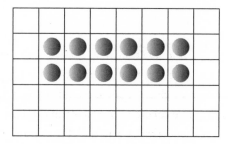

The rectangles that can be adopted by the number 12 (and by extension all rectangular numbers), are defined by the product of their factors when these can be grouped into two. In this case, for 12, we have:

$$3 \cdot 4 = 12,$$
$$2 \cdot 6 = 12.$$

Hence, there are two different ways. What about 15? There is only one way, as only two of its factors give 15 when multiplied together 15 ($3 \cdot 5 = 15$).

Surds

Surds are natural numbers without an exact square root. They are given this name because it is as if they don't make sense. One example: $\sqrt{2}$ (the square root of 2) cannot be simplified to a whole number, and hence is a surd. However, $\sqrt{4}$ (the square root of 4) can be simplified to 2; hence it is not a surd.

Automorphic numbers

Automorphic numbers are those that appear at the end of their own square. Leaving to one side the trivial cases of 0 and 1, 5 and 6 are the only single-digit automorphic numbers; the two-digit automorphic numbers are 25, whose square is 625, and 76, whose square is 5,776. The three-digit automorphic numbers are 376 and 625.

These numbers give the impression that, in spite of the transformation they undergo when squared, they preserve something of their own identity by remaining present in the new number. There is a maximum of two automorphic numbers for any number with a given number of digits, one ending in 5 and the other ending in 6. There are no more. However, normally there is only one. The only example of a four-digit automorphic number is 9,376. The only five-digit automorphic number is 90,625.

Trimorphic numbers

Trimorphic numbers are similar to automorphic numbers; however, this time, the property applies to their cube: $4^3 = 64$; $24^3 = 13,824$; $249^3 = 15,438,249$. All automorphic numbers are also trimorphic.

Oblong numbers

Oblong numbers (also referred to as pronic) are numbers of the form $n(n + 1)$, where n is a natural number. The explanation is simple: they are the results of the multiplication of two consecutive numbers. The nth oblong number is equal to twice the nth triangular number, or n units more than the nth square number. The first oblong numbers are: 0, 2, 6, 12, 20, 30, 42, 56, 72, 90, 110, 132, 156, 182, 210, 240, 272, 306 ...

They are called oblong because they can be represented in the following way:

Decagonal numbers

These are numbers that can be arranged in such a way that their shape represents a decagon.

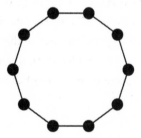

The decagonal number for a number n is given by the formula: $4n^2 - 3n$, for $n > 0$. The first decagonal numbers are: 1, 10, 27, 52, 85, 126, 175, 232, 297, 370... The numbers have alternative parities; an odd number is always followed by an even one.

Octahedral numbers

Similar to decagonal numbers, octahedral numbers can be graphically represented as an octahedron or two square pyramids joined at the base. These numbers can be calculated using the following formula:

$$O_n = \frac{1}{3}(2n^3 + n).$$

The first octahedral numbers are: 1, 6, 19, 44, 85, 146, 231, 344, 489... In 1850, Sir Frederick Pollock conjectured that any number is the sum of a maximum of seven octahedral numbers.

Emirp numbers

'Emirp' is prime spelt backwards. Jeremiah P. Farrell used the term to refer to non-palindromic numbers that were also prime numbers if the order of their digits was reversed. The last emirp year was 1979. The next will be 3011. Unfortunately, in both cases, one digit is repeated, and number hunters are more interested in 'emirp' numbers with digits that are not repeated, referred to as 'emirp no-rep'. The first terms in the series are: 13, 17, 31, 37, 71, 73, 79, 97, 107... It goes without saying that the set of 'emirp no-rep' numbers is finite, as any number with more than 10 digits contains repetitions.

There is only one six-digit cyclic emirp. If we move the first digit to the last place and repeat the operation with all the digits, the resulting permutations are all emirp. This number, the only one of its kind, is 193,939. Put another way, writing the digits in a circle, starting with any digit and following the circle in both directions will always give a six-digit prime. There are no emirp cycles with four, five or seven digits.

Weird numbers

These are numbers with divisors that add up to more than the number itself, but the number cannot be obtained from any combination of divisors. They are referred to as 'weird' because they really are. The only weird numbers below 10,000 are: 70; 836; 4,030; 5,830; 7,192; 7,912; and 9,272. Note that all of these are even. The mathematician Paul Erdös offered \$10 for the first odd example and \$25 dollars for proof that such numbers did not exist. Today, it is still not known if there are odd weird numbers, but if they do exist, we know they must be less than $2^{32} \approx 4 \cdot 10^9$.

Mirror numbers

Two natural numbers are referred to as mirror products when their two mirror images give the same product. For example, $23 \cdot 64 = 46 \cdot 32$.

Other pairs of mirror numbers include:

$$42 \cdot 36 = 24 \cdot 63.$$
$$21 \cdot 36 = 12 \cdot 63.$$
$$21 \cdot 48 = 12 \cdot 84.$$
$$31 \cdot 26 = 13 \cdot 62.$$

$$39 \cdot 62 = 93 \cdot 26.$$
$$69 \cdot 32 = 96 \cdot 23.$$
$$41 \cdot 28 = 14 \cdot 82.$$
$$36 \cdot 84 = 63 \cdot 48.$$
$$86 \cdot 34 = 68 \cdot 43.$$

Untouchable numbers

Untouchable numbers are all natural numbers that are not the sum of the proper divisors of any number. For example, the numbers 52 and 88 are untouchable

Numbers with names and surnames

Kaprekar numbers

Squaring a Kaprekar number and taking a certain number of digits from the right, gives the original number when added to the remaining number on the left. For example: $297^2 = 88,209$; its parts: $88 + 209 = 297$. Hence, 297 is a Kaprekar number.

The first Kaprekar numbers are 1, 9, 45, 55, 99, 297, 703, 999, 2,223, 2,728, 4,950, 5,050, 7,272, 7,777... Many consecutive numbers from the Kaprekar series give round numbers when added. For example: $1 + 9 = 10$; $45 + 55 = 100$; $297 + 703 = 1000$; $4,950 + 5,050 = 10,000$, etc.

The number 142,857 is a Kaprekar number: $142,857^2 = 20,408,122,449$. Separating the number into two parts and adding them together gives: $20,408 + 122,449 = 142,857$. The smallest 10-digit Kaprekar number is:

$$1,111,111,111.$$

These numbers, full of shapes and sonorous shells, are named after the Indian mathematician Shri Dattatreya Ramachandra Kaprekar (1905–1986).

Catalan numbers

Catalan numbers (named after the Belgian mathematician Eugène Charles Catalan) are the sequence of numbers given by the formula:

$$\frac{1}{n+1}\binom{2n}{n}.$$

This gives 1, 2, 5, 14, 42, 132, 429, 1,430, 4,862, 16,796, 58,786, 208,012... This apparently meaningless series has been shown to be useful for answering subtle questions posed by both mathematicians themselves and scientists. For example, how many ways can a regular polygon with n sides be divided into $(n-2)$ triangles, if each orientation is counted separately? The answer is given by the Catalan numbers.

Eugène Charles Catalan (1814–1894) discovered the numbers that bear his name for solving problems from the field of combinatorics.

Another example, how many ways can parentheses be placed around a sequence of $n + 1$ letters such that there are two letters inside each set of parentheses? For *ab* there is just one way: (*ab*). For *abc* there are two ways: (*ab*)*c* and *a*(*bc*). For *abcd* there are five ways..., and so on, following the Catalan numbers.

Sophie Germain numbers

Sophie Germain numbers, named in honour of their discoverer, the French mathematician Marie-Sophie Germain, are a special type of prime number

– those that give another prime number when multiplied by 2 and adding 1. In symbol notation, p is a Sophie Germain prime if $2p + 1$ is also prime. The smallest Sophie Germain prime that exists is 2, as $2 \cdot 2 + 1 = 5$, which is also prime. The next is 3, as $2 \cdot 3 + 1 = 7$. For a long time, the largest known Sophie Germain number was $9,402,702,309 \cdot 10^{3000} + 1$. Doubling this number and adding 1 gives a prime number. The current record for Sophie Germain prime numbers was set in February 2016:

$$2,618,163,402,417 \cdot 2^{1,290,000} - 1.$$

It has 388,342 digits, and, like all Sophie Germain primes, doubling it and adding 1 gives another prime number.

$$2,618,163,402,417 \cdot 2^{1,290,001} - 1.$$

It is assumed, even if it has not been proven, that there is an endless number of Sophie Germain primes, just like prime numbers.

Lychrel numbers

A Lychrel number is a natural number that does not form a palindromic number when the reverse of its digits is added iteratively. This process is referred to as the 196 algorithm, as 196 is the first natural number that does not comply with this condition.

A palindrome is normally derived using simple arithmetic rules: given a number, we add the number that is formed by the reverse of its digits. If the result is not a palindrome, we apply the process again to the new number. After a certain number of steps, we will end up with a palindrome. For example:

$56 + 65 = 121$, for step one.
$139 + 931 = 1,070$; $1,070 + 0701 = 1,771$, for step two.

However, this technique does not always work. The first natural number for which it does not work is 196, which is the root of its peculiarity. These numbers, which are irreducible to a palindrome by means of adding their inverse, are referred to as Lychrel numbers, in honour of the mathematician Wade Van Landingham (Lychrel is an anagram of the name of his partner, Cheryl).

To this day, the only known Lychrel number remains 196; however it is thought there are many.

Fibonacci numbers

These are the numbers of the well-known series, famous for having appeared in so many books and films, devised by Leonardo de Pisa, better known as Fibonacci (son of Bonaccio). The numbers are represented as F_n and follow the sequence: 1, 1, 2, 3, 5, 8, 13..., where each term is the sum of the two previous terms, with the exception of the second 1.

However, let's consider this numerical series, without doubt the most famous in the world of mathematics, in greater detail. It first appeared in the book *Liber Abaci*, by Fibonacci (c. 1175–1250) in relation to calculating the growth of breeding rabbits. Fibonacci asked how many pairs of rabbits would be produced in a year, starting with just a single pair if the pair gave birth to a new pair that became fertile from the second month? Assuming the rabbits reproduce without limits, the number of rabbits born at the end of each month is given by the peculiar sequence:

$$1, 1, 2, 3, 5, 8, 13, 21, 34, 55...$$

Graphically, the progression of the birth of the rabbits is:

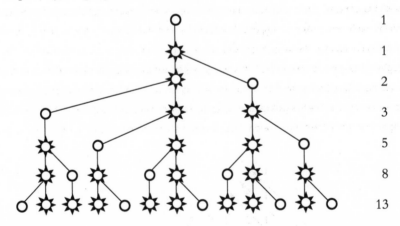

	1
	1
	2
	3
	5
	8
	13

Circles with stars represent pairs in a fertile period and the normal circles represent pairs when they are not fertile. On the right, note how the Fibonacci sequence, which was given its name by Édouard Lucas in 1877, develops at the end of each month.

This series has a number of properties that have made it the most widely studied numeric series. The most important, in our opinion, is its relationship with the golden ratio (Φ). We can see this by calculating the proportion of dividing each number by the previous term:

$$F_2/F_1 = 1/1 = 1.$$
$$F_3/F_2 = 2/1 = 2.$$
$$F_4/F_3 = 3/2 = 1.5.$$
$$F_5/F_4 = 5/3 = 1.6666...$$
$$F_6/F_5 = 8/5 = 1.6.$$
$$F_7/F_6 = 13/8 = 1.625.$$
$$F_8/F_7 = 21/13 = 1.61538.$$

As we work our way along the series, we grow increasingly close to the golden ratio (1.61803...). In fact, the limit of the aforementioned series is the golden ratio:

$$\lim_{n \to \infty} F_n / F_{n-1} = \Phi.$$

THE FIBONACCI SERIES AND PASCAL'S TRIANGLE

Pascal's triangle was, contrary to what one might expect from its name, not discovered by Pascal, although the French thinker was responsible for introducing it to the West. It is known that in ancient China, Chia Hsien used the triangle for extracting the square and cubic roots of numbers. It is also thought to have been known to the 11th-century Persian mathematician Omar Khayyam, author of the famous *Rubaiyat*, who claimed he had a method for extracting square and cubic roots. However, here we show this unique triangle's relationship to the Fibonacci series. Drawing lines that cut across the triangle, as shown in the drawing below, these lines give the numbers of the Fibonacci series in order.

Tribonacci numbers (or sequence)

These are numeric elements of the series constructed in the style of the Fibonacci series but using sums of 3:

$$A(1) = 1.$$
$$A(2) = 1.$$
$$A(3) = 2.$$
$$A(4) = 4.$$
$$A(5) = 7.$$

And the recurrence formula is:

$$A(n) = A(n-3) + A(n-2) + A(n-1) \text{ for } n > 3.$$

The first terms are: $1, 1, 2, 4, 7, 13, 24...$

Mersenne numbers

Mersenne numbers, represented by the number M are all the numbers calculated using the formula: $M_p = 2^p - 1$, where p is a natural number. They were discovered by the French mathematician Marin Mersenne (1588–1648).

If p is a composite number, $M_p = 2^p - 1$ is also composite.

Mersenne numbers are extremely useful when it comes to calculating very large prime numbers, as they are calculated using the above formula, where p is a prime number. However, not all Mersenne numbers produced applying the formula above are prime. In fact, at present only a few Mersenne prime numbers are known. As we have observed, the numbers are important because the formula by which they are defined has made it possible to discover the largest known prime numbers. At present, the three largest known prime numbers are Mersenne numbers:

$$2^{74,207,280} - 1, \text{ which has } 22,338,618 \text{ digits.}$$
$$2^{57,885,161} - 1, \text{ which has } 17,425,170 \text{ digits.}$$
$$2^{43,112,609} - 1, \text{ which has } 12,978,189 \text{ digits.}$$

Ulam numbers

Ulam numbers belong to the series $1, 2, 3, 4, 6, 8, 11, 13, 16, 18, 26, 28, 36, 38, 47...$ defined by the Polish mathematician Stanislaw Ulam. Starting from $a_1 = 1$, $a_2 = 2$,

PROOF THAT THE 67TH MERSENNE NUMBER ($2^{67} - 1$) CLAIMED BY THE MATHEMATICIAN TO BE PRIME IS NOT

The event took place in October 1903, at a meeting of the American Mathematical Society in New York. An unknown mathematician, F.N. Cole, was to present a paper entitled *On the Factoring of Large Numbers*. When the president of the society called the speaker to present his paper, he came up onto the stage, stood in front of the blackboard and, without saying a word, proceeded to write out the process of raising 2 to the power of 67 in chalk. When he had finished the operation, he proceeded to carefully subtract 1, still with no commentary, then moved to a clean area of the board and randomly multiplied the following sum:

$$193,707,721 \cdot 761,838,257,287.$$

The two calculations coincided. For the first time in the records of the society, the attendees applauded fiercely for the work presented to them. Cole went back to his seat without having uttered a word. Nor did anyone request an explanation.

the next terms correspond to the smallest numbers that can be uniquely expressed as the sum of two terms taken from among the previous ones. Hence,

$$3 = 1 + 2$$
$$4 = 1 + 3$$
$$6 = 4 + 2.$$

However, 5 is not a Ulam number because $5 = 2 + 3 = 1 + 4$, which means it can be expressed in two different ways.

Perrin numbers

These are numbers that belong to the sequence given by the following recurrence relation:

$$P(n) = P(n - 2) + P(n - 3) \text{ for } n > 2.$$

Hence, the first numbers are:

$$P(0) = 3, P(1) = 0, P(2) = 2, P(3) = 3 \ldots \quad \Rightarrow \quad P(n) = P(n - 2) + P(n - 3),$$

which, expressed as a numeric series, is: $3, 0, 2, 3, 2, 5, 5, 7, 10, 12, 17, 22...$ They are named after the French mathematician R. Perrin, who discovered them in 1899.

Liouville transcendental numbers

Liouville transcendental numbers have the form:

$$\sum_{n=1}^{\infty} 1/10^{n!} = 1/10 + 1/10^2 + 1/10^6 + 1/10^{24} + ...,$$

which expressed as a traditional series would be:

$$10^{-1!} + 10^{-2!} + 10^{-3!} + 10^{-4!} + ...,$$

which, written in decimal notation is:

$$0.110001000000000000000001000...$$

All the digits of the decimal expansion of this number are 0s, except for spaces that coincide with $n!$ (n factorial) to the right of the decimal point, where n is the number of consecutive numbers starting with 1. The French mathematician, Joseph Liouville, proved in 1844 that transcendental numbers can be constructed using this type of series, the example above being the simplest.

The discovery of these numbers (transcendental) has made it clear that solving various ancient geometric problems that only permit the use of a ruler and compass is impossible. Such puzzles include squaring the circle, where the 'transcendentality' of π rules out any solution.

Fermat number

These numbers are named after the French mathematician Pierre de Fermat and are positive numbers of the form:

$$F_n = 2^{2^n} + 1,$$

where n is a non-negative integer. The first four Fermat numbers are:

$$F_0 = 2^1 + 1 = 3$$
$$F_1 = 2^2 + 1 = 5$$
$$F_2 = 2^4 + 1 = 17$$
$$F_3 = 2^8 + 1 = 257$$

The numbers increase exponentially, as $F_8 = 2^{256} + 1$ is a 78-digit number.

Friedman numbers

Friedman numbers are narcissistic numbers (remember these are numbers equal to the sum of the powers of their digits all raised to the same power) that, in a given base of numbering, can be generated by all their numbers and the operators $+$, $-$, $\times$, $/$ and $\wedge$ (meaning power). The use of parenthesis is allowed to preserve the hierarchy of operations and alter the order of the numbers. It is also possible to join two digits.

The first Friedman numbers are: 25, 121, 125, 126, 127, 128, 153, 216, 289, 343, 347, 625, 688, 736, 1,022, 1,024, 1,206, 1,255, 1,260, 1,285, 1,296...

Here are some examples of the first numbers in the series:

$$25 = 5^2$$
$$121 = 11^2$$
$$125 = 5^{(1+2)}$$
$$126 = 21 \cdot 6...$$

ERDÖS NUMBERS

Paul Erdös was a Hungarian mathematician who emigrated to the United States. He was a most peculiar man. Of no fixed abode, he travelled around America giving courses and attending mathematics conferences. The prolific number of his published papers led to the establishment of the so-called 'Erdös Number' for categorising mathematicians. It worked as follows: an author who had written an article together with the mathematician himself received the number Erdös 1; authors who had published a paper with an Erdös 1 author (someone who had worked directly with the Hungarian) received the number Erdös 2. And so on, increasing the chain. The number 0 was obviously reserved for Erdös himself.

Within this category, a Friedman number is said to be 'orderly' if the digits keep their order in the calculations. The first numbers with this additional property are: 127; 343; 736; 1,285; 2,187; 2,502; 2,592; 2,737; 3,125; 3,685; 3,864; 3,972; 4,096; 6,455; 11,264; 11,664; 12,850; 13,825; 14,641; 15,552; 15,585; 15,612; 15,613... If the Friedman number is made up of all the digits from 1 to 9, it receives the name pandigital. Examples of pandigital Friedman numbers include:

$$123,456,789 = ((86 + 2 \cdot 7)^5 - 91)/3^4 \text{ and}$$
$$987,654,321 = (8 \cdot (97 + 6/2)^5 + 1)/3^4.$$

If we allow the use of factorials and roots, Friedman numbers are extended to include numbers as curious as:

$$1,296 = \sqrt{2\sqrt[9]{6}^{\frac{1}{2}}}.$$

$$1,944 = \sqrt{\sqrt{\left(1\sqrt{9!}\right)^{4!}}}/4!.$$

$$2,742 = \sqrt{\sqrt{\left(\sqrt{2 \cdot 7}\right)^{4!}}} - 2.$$

$$2,746 = 2 + \sqrt{\left(7\sqrt{4}\right)^6}.$$

The Champernowne number

The following number is known as the Champerowne number (also referred to as the constant C_{10}, to indicate it is in base 10): 0.123456789 10 11 12... It is named after its discoverer, D.G. Champernowne (1912–2000). Its digits are all the natural numbers in an ordered sequence (a space has been left after the number 9 to make it easier to see the sequence). This is a number in which all possible numeric blocks of the same length occur with the same probability. The constant is a transcendental number (its continuous fraction never ends), as shown by Kurt Mahler.

The previous number is in base 10, but it is possible to find Champernowne constants in any base of numbering. For example, this is what the constant looks like in base 2:

$$C_2 = 0.1 \ 10 \ 11 \ 100 \ 101 \ 110 \ 111.$$

For a given base, the constant can be expressed as an infinite sum of the type:

$$C_b = \sum_{n=1}^{\infty} \frac{\sum_{k=b^{n-1}}^{b^n-1} kb^{-n(k-(b^{n-1}-1))}}{b \sum_{k=0}^{n-1} k(b-1)b^{k-1}}.$$

Pell numbers

Pell numbers, in honour of John Pell (1611–1685), had been discovered previously, but the British mathematician was the first to name them. They are numbers that belong to a curious series made up of the denominators of successive approximations to the square root of 2 using continuous fractions. The sequence of these approximations begins $1/1, 3/2, 7/5, 17/12, 41/29\ldots$ Hence the sequence of Pell numbers begins $1, 2, 5, 12$ and $29\ldots$

The numerators of these continuous fractions are half the so-called Pell–Lucas numbers (after Édouard Lucas), which follow the series $2, 6, 14, 34, 82\ldots$, precisely double the values of the numerators of the aforementioned fractions.

Both series can be calculated using a recurrence relation similar to that used for the Fibonacci numbers. The two sequences grow exponentially, in proportion to the 'silver ratio' $1 + \sqrt{2}$. In addition to providing approximations for the square root of 2 ($\sqrt{2}$), the series of Pell numbers can also be used to find triangular numbers, as well as for solving certain enumeration problems in combinatorics.

Markov numbers

Markov numbers are positive numbers x, y and z that are part of the solution of the Markov Diophantine equation:

$$x^2 + y^2 + z^2 = 3xyz.$$

The first Markov numbers are: $1, 2, 5, 13, 29, 34, 89, 169, 194\ldots$ These numbers make up the coordinates of the so-called Markov 'triplets'.

$(1, 1, 1), (1, 1, 2), (1, 2, 5), (1, 5, 13), (2, 5, 29), (1, 13, 34), (1, 34, 89), (2, 29, 169),$
$(5, 13, 194), (1, 89, 233), (5, 29, 433), (89, 233, 610),$ etc.

A portrait of the Russian mathematician Andrei Markov (1856–1922), who made brilliant contributions to number theory and probability.

which can be represented visually as follows, where each forking corresponds to a Markov triplet. There is an infinite number of Markov numbers and triplets:

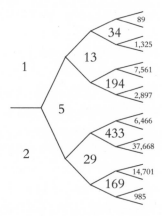

Poulet numbers

A Poulet (or Fermatian) number is a number n that satisfies the following congruence:

$$2^{n-1} \equiv 1 \ (\text{mod } n).$$

Poulet numbers include all odd prime numbers, Fermat numbers, Mersenne numbers and Carmichael numbers.

QUENEAU HYPERPRIMES

The French author Raymond Queneau christened a special type of prime number as hyperprime. A right hyperprime is a prime number when if one or more digits is removed from its right (or from the left in the case of a left hyperprime), the remaining part is still a prime number. According to Queneau, the largest right hyperprime is 1,979,339,339, whereas the largest known left hyperprime is 12,953. It is not known if left hyperprimes necessarily have a finite number of digits. Finally, there are hyperprimes that are both left and right, such as 3,137.

The first Poulet numbers are: 341, 561, 645, 1,105, 1,387... (the second and fourth are also Carmichael numbers).

Super-Poulet numbers

A super-Poulet number is a Poulet number for which each of its divisors (d) divides separately:

$$2^d - 2.$$

For example, 341 is a super-Poulet number with positive divisors $(1, 11, 31, 341)$ that satisfy the aforementioned condition:

$(2^{11} - 2) / 11 = 2{,}046 / 11 = 186,$

$(2^{31} - 2) / 31 = 2{,}147{,}483{,}646 / 31 = 69{,}273{,}666,$

$(2^{341} - 2) / 341 = 13{,}136{,}332{,}798{,}696{,}798{,}888{,}899{,}954{,}724{,}741{,}608{,}669{,}335{,}164,$
$206{,}654{,}835{,}981{,}818{,}117{,}894{,}215{,}788{,}100{,}763{,}407{,}304{,}286{,}671{,}514{,}789{,}484{,}550.$

The super-Poulet numbers below 10,000 are: 341 $(11 \cdot 31)$, 1,387 $(19 \cdot 73)$, 2,047 $(23 \cdot 89)$, 2,701 $(37 \cdot 73)$, 3,277 $(29 \cdot 113)$, 4,033 $(37 \cdot 109)$, 4,369 $(17 \cdot 257)$, 4,681 $(31 \cdot 151)$, 5,461 $(43 \cdot 127)$, 7,957 $(73 \cdot 109)$ and 8,321 $(53 \cdot 157)$. The numbers in parentheses are their factors.

Carmichael numbers

Carmichael numbers are composite numbers n that satisfy the following congruence:

$$a^{n-1} \equiv 1 \ (\mathrm{mod}\ n)$$

for all integers a that are prime relative to n.

The Carmichael numbers are named after the mathematician Robert Daniel Carmichael, who was the first to study them. They are pseudo-prime in any base. The first Carmichael numbers are: 561, 1,105, 1,729, 2,465, 2,821, 6,601, 8,911, 10,585... Let us consider the first:

$$n = 561 = 3 \cdot 11 \cdot 17$$

Thus it is not prime. However, $a^{560} - 1$ is divisible by 561 for any a coprime with 561.

Leyland numbers

In number theory, Leyland numbers (named after their discoverer, the English mathematician Paul Leyland) are numbers of the form $x^y + y^x$, where x and y are greater than 1. The first Leyland numbers are: 8, 17, 32, 54, 57, 100, 145, 177, 320, 368, 512... Let us now see how the first two are calculated:

For x and $y = 2$ $\Rightarrow$ $2^2 + 2^2 = 4 + 4 = 8.$
For x and $y = 2$ and 3 $\Rightarrow$ $2^3 + 3^2 = 8 + 9 = 17.$

And so on... It is an important requirement that both x and y are greater than 1, otherwise all numbers would be Leyland numbers in the form $x^1 + 1^x$.

The first prime Leyland numbers are: 17, 593, 32,993, 2,097,593..., which correspond to the forms: $3^2 + 2^3$, $9^2 + 2^9$, $15^2 + 2^{15}$, $21^2 + 2^{21}$... The largest prime Leyland number is $2,638^{4,405} + 4,405^{2,638}$, which has 15,071 digits.

Cullen numbers

These are numbers of the form: $n \cdot 2^n + 1$. They were discovered by the Irish mathematician James Cullen and are prime for the values of n: 1, 141, 4,713, 5,795, 6,611 and 18,496. They are composite for all other values up to $n < 30,000$.

The smallest prime Cullen number is $141 \cdot 2^{141} + 1$. The next ones are generated following this model: the previously specified values $n \cdot 2^n + 1$ for suitable values of n. There is a hypothesis (conjecture) that Cullen prime numbers are infinite; however, this has not been proven.

Woodall numbers

A Woodall number is a number of the form $(n \cdot 2^n - 1)$. The smallest Woodall numbers are: 1, 7, 23, 63, 159, 383, 895... They are named after H. J. Woodall, the English mathematician who defined them.

Bell numbers

Bell numbers, named in honour of the Scottish mathematician Eric Temple Bell, are the terms of the series 1, 2, 5, 15, 52, 203, 877, 4,140, 21,147, 115,975, 678,570, 4,213,597...

They represent the different ways of putting n labelled balls into n indistinguishable boxes. Hence, the symbols a, b and c can be placed in three boxes (possibly empty) in five different ways: (abc), $(a)(bc)$, $(b)(ac)$, $(c)(ab)$ and $(a)(b)(c)$.

They also represent the different ways of expressing a composite number that is the product of n different prime factors. In the case of the number $30 = 2 \cdot 3 \cdot 5$ there are five different ways of decomposing the product: $30 = 6 \cdot 5 = 3 \cdot 10 = 30 \cdot 1 = 15 \cdot 2 = 2 \cdot 3 \cdot 5$.

The Copeland–Erdös number

This number is the result of joint work by the mathematicians Arthur Herbert Copeland and Paul Erdös. The number is:

$$0.235711131719232931\ldots,$$

where all prime numbers appear consecutively after the comma.

It is an irrational constant (a number that cannot be expressed as a fraction m/n, where m and n are integers). Applying the Dirichlet theorem of primes in arithmetic progressions, it can be deduced that for each m there are prime numbers of the form:

$$k10^{m+1} + 1.$$

This also indicates there are prime numbers with decimal expressions that contains at least m 0s followed by a 1, which in turn implies the Copeland–Erdös constant has arbitrarily long sequences of 0s followed by a 1. Therefore, it is not periodic and never ends. This means it is irrational. The constant is given by the formula:

$$\sum_{n=1}^{\circ} p(n) 10^{-\left(n+\sum_{k=1}^{n}\left\lceil \log_{10} p(k) \right\rceil\right)}$$

where $p(n)$ is the nth prime number.

Chen prime numbers

A prime number p is said to be a Chen number if $p + 2$ is prime or the product of two prime numbers. The even number $2p + 2$ satisfies the Chen theorem. The mathematician after whom the numbers are named, Chen Jingrun, proved in 1966 that there are infinitely many primes of this type.

The first Chen primes are: 2, 3, 5, 7, 11, 13, 17, 19, 23, 29, 31, 37, 41, 47, 53, 59, 67, 71, 83... And the first non-prime Chen numbers are: 43, 61, 73, 79, 97, 103, 151, 163...

Curiously, there is a magic square with Chen primes, devised by Rudolf Ondrejka:

17	89	71
113	59	5
47	29	101

It is a magic 3 × 3 square with the magic constant 177.

The largest known Chen prime is $65{,}516{,}468{,}355 \cdot 2^{333{,}333} - 1$, which has 100,355 digits.

Smith numbers

These are integers for which the sum of their digits is equal to the sum of the digits of their prime factors, without using exponents or repeating the numbers as many times as is necessary. For example, 666 is a Smith number (note that all the digits are added separately and hence the prime factor 37 is $3 + 7$):

$$666 = 2 \cdot 3 \cdot 3 \cdot 37,$$
$$6 + 6 + 6 = 2 + 3 + 3 + 3 + 7.$$

The first Smith numbers are: 4, 22, 27, 58, 85, 94, 121, 166, 202, 265, 274, 319, 346, 355, 378, 382, 391, 438, 454, 483, 517, 526, 535, 562, 576, 588, 627, 634, 636, 645, 648, 654, 663, 666, 690, 706, 728, 729, 762, 778, 825, 852, 861, 895, 913, 915, 922, 958, 985, 1,086... Curiously, they were not discovered by a mathematician named Smith, but by Albert Wilanski, at the University of Lehigh, who realised the telephone number of his brother-in-law (named Harold Smith) had the aforementioned peculiar property. His discovery was made in 1982.

Lucas numbers

Named after the French mathematician who discovered them, Édouard Lucas, these are numbers from the sequence: 1, 3, 4, 7, 11, 18, 29, 47, 76, 123, 199, 322... that are closely related to the Fibonacci numbers. Each term is the sum of the two preceding numbers and the ratio of its terms tends to the golden ratio.

The formula to find the nth term in the series is extremely similar to that used for the Fibonacci series, as the Lucas number is 2 for $n = 0$ and 1 for $n = 1$. From this point on, they obey the rule: $L(n - 1) + L(n + 1)$ for $n > 1$.

Their relationship with the Fibonacci numbers is given by the formula:

$$L_n = F_{n-1} + F_{n+1}.$$

Édouard Lucas (1842–1891) analysed the Fibonacci series in depth and created his own numeric sequence.

The Graham number

The Graham number, named after the mathematician Ronald L. Graham, is of the form $3 \uparrow \uparrow \uparrow \uparrow 3$, where $3 \uparrow 3$ means 3 cubed, and is $G = f^{64}(4)$, where $f(n) = 3^n \uparrow 3$. Hence, it has 64 layers of factors of the form $3 \uparrow \uparrow \ldots \uparrow \uparrow 3$. Such a number cannot be expressed in the conventional way using powers and powers of powers, as even if all the matter in the Universe was transformed into ink, it would not be possible to write it down. It is for this reason that they use this special notation devised by Donald Knuth.

In this special notation, $3 \uparrow 3$ represents, as we have noted, 3 cubed, as expressed in computer printouts. $3 \uparrow \uparrow 3$ represents $3 \uparrow (3 \uparrow 3)$, or $3 \uparrow 27$, an enormous number: $3 \uparrow 27 = 7,625,597,484,987$, but which can be easily expressed as a tower of three numbers: $3^{3^{13}}$. However, $3 \uparrow \uparrow \uparrow 3 = 3 \uparrow \uparrow (3 \uparrow \uparrow 3)$ is already $3 \uparrow \uparrow 7,625,597,484,987 = 3 \uparrow 3 \uparrow 3 \uparrow 3 \uparrow \ldots \ldots 7,625,597,484,987$ times. Even using the new system of notation $3 \uparrow \uparrow \uparrow \uparrow 3 = 3 \uparrow \uparrow \uparrow (3 \uparrow \uparrow \uparrow 3)$, the tower of exponents is unimaginably large.

For many years it was the largest number ever used in a mathematical proof, and hence appears in the *Guinness Book of Records*. (However, today even larger numbers have been used in other mathematical proofs, for example by the US mathematician Harvey Friedman for certain approximations to Kruskal's theorem.) The Graham number is much larger even than a googol or a googolplex (numbers we shall explain further on); in fact, it is so large that cannot be written out; however, it is known that its last digits are: ...2464195387.

The web page of the Department of Mathematics at the University of California in honour of Ron Graham, the creator of a number whose proportions are hard to imagine.

The Euler–Mascheroni constant

This number, better known as 'Euler's constant', is represented using the lower case Greek letter: γ, and is a numeric constant that mainly appears in number theory. It is defined as the limit of the difference between the harmonic series and the natural logarithm; in mathematical notation:

$$\gamma = \lim_{n \to \infty} \left[\sum_{k=1}^{n} \frac{1}{k} - \log(n) \right] = \int_{1}^{\infty} \left(\frac{1}{[x]} - \frac{1}{x} \right) dx.$$

Its approximate value is:

$$\gamma = 0.57721\ 56649\ 01532\ 86060\ 65120\ 90082\ 40243\ 1...$$

Euler calculated the number to its 16th decimal place and called it *gamma*. It is still unknown if the number is irrational, less still transcendental; however, it is known that if it is a rational number of the form a/b, b would need to be greater than $10^{10,000}$.

Like any number of interest, there have been those who have sought out its decimal places. Alexander J. Yee was able to calculate 116 million digits of the constant on a laptop. Yee's computer was an Intel Core Duo running at 1.6 GHz with Windows XP; very average by today's standards. It took 38 hours to carry out the calculation and another 48 to check it.

Feigenbaum numbers

Discovered by the mathematician Mitchell Feigenbaum in 1975, Feigenbaum numbers (or constants) are two real numbers that express quotients that appear in the bifurcation diagrams of chaos theory. The first Feigenbaum constant is defined as the limit of the quotients between two successive intervals of the bifurcation:

$$\delta = \lim_{n \to \infty} \frac{\mu_{n+1} - \mu_{n}}{\mu_{n+2} - \mu_{n+1}}.$$

And its approximate value is:

$$\delta \approx 4.66920160910299067185320382...$$

The second constant is defined as the limit of the ratio between two successive distances between the closest branches to x_m (the maximum of the function f):

$$\alpha = \lim_{n \to \infty} \frac{d_n}{d_{n+1}}.$$

Its approximate value is:

$$\alpha \approx 2.502907875095892822283902873218\ldots$$

These constants are used for special applications in dynamic systems. Both numbers, which are real numbers, are believed to be transcendental (a type of irrational number that is not the root of a polynomial with whole number coefficients), although this has not been proven.

Harshad numbers

Harshad numbers are integers that are divisible by the sum of their digits in a given base. They were defined by the Indian mathematician D.R. Kaprekar. The word *harshad* comes from Sanskrit and means 'great joy'. They are also known as Niven numbers, as it was the American mathematician Ivan Morton Niven who presented them in an article published in 1997.

All integers between 0 and a given base are Harshad numbers. In base 10 they are the numbers from 1 to 9. In bases with more digits, the Harshad numbers are: 10, 12, 18, 20, 24, 27, 30, 36, 40, 42, 45, 48…

The Kaprekar number 6,174 is also a Harshad number, as it is divisible by the sum of its digits.

$$6{,}174 \,/\, (6+1+7+4) \;\Rightarrow\; 6{,}174 \,/\, 18 = 343.$$

UHLER'S NUMBER

Uhler's number has 1,001 digits: 450! (450 factorial). It was calculated in the 1950s by the mathematician Horace Uhler. As we have seen in the chapter on notable numbers, it is also known as the 'factorial of One Thousand and One Nights'.

The Ruth–Aaron pairs

Ruth–Aaron pairs are pairs of consecutive numbers (714 and 715) with curious properties. Carl Pomerance, who discovered them, instead of using his own name, called them Ruth–Aaron numbers in honour of two baseball players who achieved records in the baseball league that coincided with the numbers 714 and 715.

This pair of numbers has interesting arithmetic properties that gives it great esoteric and symbolic potential. Its unique properties are:

1. Its product is also the product of the first seven prime numbers: $714 \cdot 715 = 2 \cdot 3 \cdot 5 \cdot 7 \cdot 11 \cdot 13 \cdot 17$.

2. The sum of the prime factors of 714 is equal to the sum of the prime factors of 715: $714 = 2 \cdot 3 \cdot 7 \cdot 17$; $715 = 5 \cdot 11 \cdot 13$, and hence, $2 + 3 + 7 + 17 = 5 + 11 + 13$.

Apéry's constant

Apéry's constant is defined as the number $\varsigma(3)$, and is equal to:

$$\varsigma(3) = 1 + \frac{1}{2^3} + \frac{1}{3^3} + \frac{1}{4^3} + \dots$$

where ς is Riemann's zeta function. Its value is:

$$\varsigma(3) = 1,20205\ 69031\ 59594\ 28539\ 97381\ 61511\ 44999\ 07649\ 86292\dots$$

The constant is named after the Greek–French mathematician Roger Apéry, who proved the number is irrational in 1977.

O'Really's number

The Irish writer Lambert O'Really invented a unique number for one of his novels:

$$12233344445555566666677777778888888999999999.$$

As is clear, the number is finite and contains, in order, all the natural numbers from 1 to 9, with each repeated as many times as its cardinality: 1 appears once, 2 twice, 3 three times, and so on, until 9, which appears nine times. O'Really could have gone further and created an inexhaustible number, continuing after the ninth 9 with the number 10 repeated ten times, 11 eleven times, 12 twelve times and so on, *ad infinitum*.

A cryptographic number

The following number: 114,381,625,757,888,867,669,235,779,976,146,612,010, 218,296,721,242,362,562,561,842,935,706,935,245,733,897,830,597,123,563, 958,705,058,989,075,147,599,290,026,879,543,541 was used by Shamir, Rivest and Adelman as the key for a system of cryptography. It is referred to as 'R 129', in reference to the number of digits. The authors challenged the world to find the two prime factors of R 129 that could be used to decipher the encrypted message. They were convinced of the absolute security of the message, persuaded the number would never be deciphered. However, in 1993 a team of more than 600 academics and enthusiasts from throughout the world began to attack the number methodically, using the Internet to combine their computing power. In less than a year, they were able to factorise the number into two prime numbers, one with 65 digits and the other with 64. The deciphered R 129 message was: *The magic words are squeamish and ossifrage.* Subsequently, in 1996, another number of this form, known as R 130 (because it had 130 digits) was factorised by a Dutch team into two prime factors, both with 65 digits.

GARCÍA'S NUMBERS

Given that so many mathematicians have their own numbers, I have come up with my own, albeit without a great deal of originality:

$$0.2483225681922097152\ldots$$

Starting with the first number after the decimal, the number contains the first prime number, followed by the next even number, and an infinite sequence in which the next term is formed by multiplying the two previous ones. This is clearer if the number is represented using parentheses:

$$0.24(8)(32)(256)(8192)(2097152)\ldots$$

The numbers in parentheses are the results of multiplying the two previous numbers.

Other-worldly numbers

This is a series of numbers that lie beyond the imagination. They are quaternions, octonions and sedenions.

Quaternions are an extension of the real numbers, similar to complex numbers, with which they share certain properties. However, while complex numbers extend the real numbers by adding an imaginary unit i, such that $i^2 = -1$, quaternions are an extension in a similar fashion by adding the imaginary units: i, j and k to the real numbers, such that:

$$i^2 = j^2 = k^2 = ijk = -1.$$

This can be summarised in the following multiplication table, referred to as Cayley's table.

	1	i	j	k
1	1	i	j	k
i	i	-1	k	$-j$
j	j	$-k$	-1	i
k	k	j	$-i$	-1

In this way, $1, i, j$ and k are the 'bases' of the components of a quaternion. Quaternions were devised by William Hamilton in 1843, who sought ways to extend the complex numbers to higher dimensions. He failed in his attempt to create complex numbers in three dimensions, but was able to do so in four, referring to them as quaternions. The solution to his long search occurred to him one day when he was out with his wife. The mathematician describes his inspiration as follows: "They [quaternions] started into life, or light, full grown, on Monday, 16 October 1843, as I was walking with Lady Hamilton to Dublin, and came up to Brougham Bridge, which my boys have since called the Quaternion Bridge. That is to say, I then and there felt the galvanic circuit of thought close; and the sparks which fell from it were the fundamental equations between i, j, k [the numbers that play the role of i in the complex numbers], exactly such as I have used them ever since… But then it is fair to say that this was because I felt a problem to have been at that moment solved – an intellectual want relieved – which had haunted me for at least fifteen years before."

THE GOOGOL

There are numbers so large that an immense number of digits would be required to write them down. This has led to the invention of certain words to help express them. These include the googol: a 1 followed by a hundred 0s, or 10^{100}. Googols are used to describe enormous quantities, such as the number of grains of sand in a desert, or the distance of the Earth from far-off planets or remote galaxies. The name was first coined by the mathematician Edward Kasner, who confessed that his inspiration came from a nephew who was nine years old. The child was also responsible for the name given to an even larger number, the googolplex, defined as a 1 followed by as many 0s as it is possible to write before your hand gets tired. With greater precision, his uncle defined it as 10 raised to the power of a googol: 10^{googol} or $10^{10^{100}}$.

Octonions, for their part, can be defined as the non-associative extension of quaternions. They were discovered by John T. Graves in 1843, and at the same time, and independently, by Arthur Cayley, who published his discovery in 1845, hence they are frequently referred to as Cayley numbers.

Octonions form an eight-dimensional algebra over the real numbers. Each octonion represents a linear combination of base 1, e_1, e_2, e_3, e_4, e_5, e_6, e_7. The rules for multiplying octonions are given in the table below:

·	1	e_1	e_2	e_3	e_4	e_5	e_6	e_7
1	1	e_1	e_2	e_3	e_4	e_5	e_6	e_7
e_1	e_1	-1	e_4	e_7	$-e_2$	e_6	$-e_5$	$-e_3$
e_2	e_2	$-e_4$	-1	e_5	e_1	$-e_3$	e_7	$-e_6$
e_3	e_3	$-e_7$	$-e_5$	-1	e_6	e_2	$-e_4$	e_1
e_4	e_4	e_2	$-e_1$	$-e_6$	-1	e_7	e_3	$-e_5$
e_5	e_5	$-e_6$	e_3	$-e_2$	$-e_7$	-1	e_1	e_4
e_6	e_6	e_5	$-e_7$	e_4	$-e_3$	$-e_1$	-1	e_2
e_7	e_7	e_3	e_6	$-e_1$	e_5	$-e_4$	$-e_2$	-1

Finally, sedenions are the equivalent of the above numbers, but with an algebra of 16 dimensions. The multiplication matrix is sufficiently complex as to warrant omission. But these numbers are truly out of this world.

Chapter 4

Notable Numbers in Non-Western Cultures

There is life in numbers outside our Western culture. It could even be argued that it was outside of the West where this fascinating Universe of digits was born. Due to the scope of this book, we shall limit ourselves to considering these numbers in the non-Western environments of India and China.

Notable numbers in India

0

The number 0 is emptiness. It is the absence of number, and its origin, as has been previously mentioned, lies in India. In Sanskrit, 'zero' is *sunya*, which means emptiness or blank, and it was already in use in the 2nd century BC. It reached the West after a long delay, through the hands of Arab scholars, who translated it as *sifr*, from which the word zero is derived. In India, the use of zero was so widespread that it even appears in poems and sacred texts. For example, in his collection of poems *Satsai*, the poet Bihari Lal praised a beautiful woman in the following words: "The point [that is painted] on her front increases her beauty tenfold, like when a 0 increases a number tenfold." This is a clear allusion to the property of zero as an arithmetic operator in

---

NEGATIVE NUMBERS IN INDIA

The Indians did not regard mathematics in the same way as they regarded geometry. Indian mathematicians were the first to recognise negative roots and both square roots of a positive number. They also multiplied positive and negative numbers, despite the fact they seemed suspicious of them. Hence, the mathematician Bhaskara, when commenting on the negative root of a second-degree equation, claimed "The second value should not be taken in this case, as it is inadequate; people do not approve of negative roots".

---

positional decimal numbering, as adding a 0 to the right of the representation of a certain number multiplies its value by 10.

The concept of 'zero' is an achievement of enormous cultural significance. It is not easy to reach it. For example, Babylonian scholars never managed to discover this sign in the sense of the 'number 0'. As we saw on the chapter on notable numbers in antiquity, the double nail or the double spike was used to refer to the 'void', but it does not appear to have been conceived in the sense of 'nothing'.

3

Just like in the West, in India 3 is a mystical number. The West probably inherited the sacred aspect of the trinity from the Indians. In India, 'three' is the *Trimurti* (which means 'trinity' in Sanskrit), made up of the creator of the Universe (Brahma) its preserver (Vishnu) and its destroyer (Shiva). According to *Samkya*, the three are aspects of a single being. The linguistic symbol for the holy trinity is the mystic syllable OM (actually, AUM; A = Brahma, U = Vishnu and M = Shiva).

In Buddhist ordination, the initiate is offered *three* robes, which are carried on stretchers; the initiate, or bonze, accepts them by touching them with a stick, not with their hand.

Brahma, Vishnu *and* Shiva *in a painting from the second half of the 18th century. Just like in the West, the number 3 and groupings into threes are extremely important in Indian thought.*

4

According to the doctrine of the Hindu *dharma*, there are four states of human existence: *brahmacharya*, *grihasta*, *vanaprastha* and *samnyasa*, three of which must be lived in chastity. Hindu theosophy also teaches that Brahma distributed men in four classes, states or hierarchies: the first is the Brahman, who, because they know the eternal truths, exercise the function of leading all men, both on Earth and in heaven; the second is Chatriya, whose vocation is earthly governance and military order; the third is Vaisya, whose function is to procure and distribute material goods; and the fourth is Sudra, born at the feet of Brahma. When all these classes remain true to their vocation and maintain their hierarchy, human order reigns and justice takes the shape of a bull firmly supported on four feet.

The number 4 is important in Buddhism. Siddharta Gautama, prince of a southern Nepalese tribe, became Buddha by achieving enlightenment (*satori*), which he achieved by understanding the Four Noble Truths: life is suffering; the origin of suffering is desire; the cessation of suffering is reaching *nirvana*, or extinguishing desire; and the path to reach it is *dharma*, fairness, the Buddhist law.

According to legend, there were also four revelations that led Guatama to take his decisive step. In one of his long solitary journeys, he met an old man; on another, a nurse; on a third, a dead man; and on a fourth, an ascetic. He considers what he has seen and heard: a decrepit and vacillating body, painful covering of wounds, a decomposing body and deep conversations with the ascetic. They reveal to him the inevitable end of all existence and the profound vanity of human passions.

5

In the *Upanishads*, it is said that the heart has five openings to the gods. The eastern opening is *prana*; the eye, the Sun, and must be meditated on as heat and food; he who knows this is brilliant and hardy. The southern opening is *vyana*; the ear, the Moon, and must be meditated on as prosperity and fame; he who knows this is prosperous and famous. The western opening is *apana*; the word, fire, and must be meditated on as the splendour of the knowledge of the Brahman; he who knows this will achieve splendour. The northern opening is *samana*; the mind, rain, and must be meditated on as fame and beauty; he who knows this is famous and beautiful. The higher opening is *udana*; the wind, space, and must be meditated on as force and greatness; he who knows this is strong and great.

These are the five characters of the Brahman, the guardians of the heavenly world. A hero will be born into the family of those who know the five characters of the *Brahman*.

In Buddhism, there is a group of five gods named the *Pañcharaksha* ('the protective quintuple'), rooted in the personification of five magic spells (*raksha*) believed to be spoken by Buddha himself. Indeed, in Buddhism, the number 5 is present in numerous guises. For example, sensory desire is based on five factors: the material forms that can be seen, which are free, desirable and attractive, which stimulate sensory desire and attract us; and those perceived by the ears, smell, taste and touch. The sensual pleasure is driven by these five 'cords of desire'.

The number 5 is present in numerous aspects of Buddhism. The illustration shows a Tibetan representation of Buddha dating back to the end of the 13th century, showing Siddharta Gautama accompanied by five images that represent the five Dhyani or five qualities.

6

The Indian *jaina* accept the Brahmic classification of the six ages of the world. We are living in the fifth age, which began around 523 BC and is characterised by suffering. This age will be followed by the sixth and final age that will last 21,000 years, at the end of which the human race will be obliterated, but the Universe goes on – for the *jaina*, the Universe is indestructible and infinite.

There were also six eminent teachers mentioned in Buddhist writing. Kasyapa maintained that acts do not obtain retribution; Maskarin Gosallputra said that the course of existence is fixed and all effort is meaningless; Ajita Kesa Kambalin claimed that the human being is composed of four elements that are divided after death; Kakuda Katyayana proposed that the human being is composed of seven permanent elements and, when somebody is murdered, there is neither murderer, victim nor murder; Sarpjayin Vairatlputra maintained there is no definitive answer to any metaphysical question; and finally, Jina Mahavira states that strict penitence is necessary in each life to pay for the sins of past ones.

8

There are eight fortunes in the Buddhist tradition, protected by the goddess Ashtaman-galadevi ('the goddess of the eight fortunes'). Her image appears surrounded by the eight Buddhist images of fortune, which are the wheel of the doctrine (*dharma-cakra*); the shell (*shanka*) as a symbol of general blessing; the water vase (*kalasha*) with the drink of immortality; the pair of fish (*matsyayugma*) as a symbol of fertility; the white parasol (*sitapatra*) as a symbol of an elevated range; the lotus (*padma*), which represents the purity of desires; the endless knot (*granthi*), as a symbol of unlimited wealth; and the parasol-standard (*dvaya*), a symbol of the triumph of the Buddhist doctrine.

In the Buddhist writings known as *Anguttara Nikaya*, it is said there is a path that leads to the cessation of suffering and that this is called the 'noble eightfold path',

EIGHT SERPENTS AND EIGHT SKULLS

The *Krodhadevatas* are dark blue or red 'terror-inspiring gods' from ancient India, with a third eye, flame-shaped hair and adornments displaying eight serpents and eight skulls. Their job is to combat the enemies of the Buddhist doctrine.

which has eight aspects within the three moral categories: *Pali* or wisdom (vision or correct understanding and thought or correct determination); *Sila* or ethical conduct (to speak correctly, act correctly and the correct measure of life); and *Samadhi* or training of the mind (correct force, being conscious at the correct moment and performing meditation).

The number 8 also abounds in Buddhism, with many divinities, such as this illustration of Tara, having eight arms, which may be a symbol of the eightfold path that leads to enlightenment.

116

In the *Upanishads*, it is stated that the person is sacrifice. The first 24 years are the libation of the morning, as the *gayatri* has 24 syllables and the morning libation is offered with a *gayatri*. The next 44 years represent the libation of midday. The *tristubh* meter has 44 syllables and the libation of midday is offered with a *tristubh*. The next 48 years are the third libation. The *jagati* meter has 48 syllables and the third libation is produced with a *jagati*. Aitareya lived for 116 years (the sum of 24 + 44 + 48). He who knows this will also live for 116 years.

COUNTING IN VERSE

In India, the period from the 5th to the 8th centuries has been defined by some Western historians as the Epoch of Poetry, as poetry appeared to permeate everything, including science and mathematics. This is how an Indian scholar stated a mathematical problem:

A necklace breaks during an amorous struggle.

And a string of pearls escapes.

A sixth falls to the ground.

A fifth remains on the bed.

A third is saved by the young lady.

The tenth part is retained by the lover.

And six pearls remain on the string.

Tell me how many pearls were on the necklace.

This is an arithmetic problem, as defined in the *Lilavati*, the famous treatise on mathematics written in verse by Bhaskaracharya (c. 1150). Another problem reproduced in poetic prose goes as follows: "Beautiful girl, with shining eyes, tell me if you have understood the method of inversion, what is the number that when multiplied by 3, adding 3/4 of the product, dividing by 7 and reducing the quotient by 1/3, multiplying the result by itself, subtracting 52, taking the square root, adding 8 and dividing by 10 gives 2?" Let us end with a third example that makes reference to the mysticism that appeared everything in India. "Two ascetics live on the summit of a mountain with a given height, the base of which is a given distance from the nearest village. To travel to the village, one of them descends and makes his way on foot. The other, who is a wizard, prefers to fly. He rises to a certain altitude and then directs himself towards the village in a straight line. How high must he rise to ensure both ascetics travel the same distance?"

India's love of enormous numbers

Indian cosmogony is replete with enormous numbers. The idea of these large numbers was to somehow represent entities or systems beyond human understanding. Its love of enormous numbers is so great that the Indians have a unit of measurement for the number 100,000 (10^5): the *lakh*, or *lac*. As well as being used for calculations, it is also used to designate people (1 lakh of people gathered together) and money (something costs 1 lakh rupees). Another unit of measurement is the *core* (abbreviated to *cr*), which represents 10^7 (10,000,000), equivalent to 100 *lakh*. Both units of measurement are commonly used in Bangladesh, India, Nepal and Pakistan. For example, 230 million rupees is written as: 'Rs 23 cr'. Let's now briefly consider some of these enormous numbers.

36,000

In Hindu mythology, the number 36,000 is used to explain the emergence of the mind, of the self, a different self beyond the bounds of the primitive brain. This can be better appreciated in this passage from the book *Ka* by Roberto Calasso: "Prajapati was alone. He didn't even know whether he existed or not. 'So to speak', *iva*. There was only the mind, *manas*. And what is peculiar about the mind is that it doesn't know whether it exists or not. But it comes before everything else. 'There is nothing before the mind.' Then, even prior to establishing whether it existed or not, the mind desired. It was constant, diffuse, undefined. Yet as though drawn to something exotic, something belonging to another species of life, it desired what was definite and separate, what had shape. A self, *atman* – that was the name it used. And the mind imagined itself as having consistency. Thinking, the mind grew red hot. It saw thirty-six thousand fires flare up, made of mind, made with mind. Suspended above the fires were thirty-six thousand cups and these too were made of mind."

2,160,000,000

For Hindus, the Universe lasts for the duration of Brahma's dream. Upon awakening, it vanishes but is born again as soon as the divinity goes to sleep again. Brahma is condemned to dream of the world, and we are his dream. The duration of these recurring dreams is 2,160 million earth years. In other versions the duration of the dreams is 4,320 million years, double the previous number.

THE TOWER OF BRAHMA

When he created the Towers of Hanoi in 1883, the mathematician Édouard Lucas recounted the following story, inspired by the enormous numbers in Indian cosmogony. In the great temple of Varanasi, beneath the dome that represents the centre of the world, there rests a bronze sheet into which three diamond needles are fixed, each of which is approximately half a metre high and the same thickness as the body of a wasp. Onto one of these needles, since creation, God placed 64 discs of pure gold, the widest disc resting on the sheet of bronze and the others, in ascending order, such that each disc was smaller than the one on which it rested; and so on until completing the 64 discs. The needle with the 64 discs was known as the Tower of Brahma. Day and night the priests transferred the discs from one diamond needle to another, in line with fixed and immutable laws that required the serving priest not to move more than one disc at a time and to place the disc on the new needle such that there were no smaller ones below it. When the 64 discs were transferred from the needle onto which they were originally placed by God onto one of the other needles, the tower, the temple and the priests themselves would turn to dust, and the world would vanish with a thunderous noise.

Mathematics can tell us how long it would take to complete this task. The Brahma priests would need $2^{64} - 1$ movements to carry it out, which in a more easily understandable form is 18,446,744,073,709,551,615 movements. Working at a rate of one movement per second, without stopping or making mistakes, and bearing in mind that there are 31,557,600 seconds in a year of 365.25 days, more than 584 thousand million years would be required: exactly 584,542,046,090 years, 7 months, 15 days, 8 hours, 54 minutes and 24 seconds. A reassuring period of time.

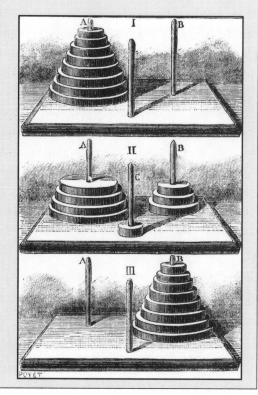

The game devised by Édouard Lucas according to an engraving at the end of the 19th century.

4,320,000,000

According to Brahmic cosmogony, the duration of the material Universe is limited, and is cyclically reproduced every *kalpa* or Brahma's day. *Bhagavad Gita*, a classic text of the Hindu religion, states that "All the planets in the Universe, from the most highly evolved to the most primitive, are places of suffering in which birth and death take place. However, for the soul that reaches *my* kingdom, oh son of Kunti, there is no more reincarnation. Men who become conscious of the Brahma's day, whose end comes after a thousand eras (*mahayuga*), and its night, which lasts many more, are those who really know the day and night." Hence, the four eras that make up a *mahayuga* tend to be repeated 1,000 times to form a Brahma's day, a unit of time equivalent to 4,320,000,000 human years.

According to this cosmogony, this is the total duration of the Universe that is created. Brahma's day corresponds to the appearance, evolution and disappearance of a world, a cycle that is followed by another cycle of 'cosmic rest' of equal duration, until a new *kalpa* begins, and so on, indefinitely. Put another way, each *kalpa* must end with the complete destruction of the Universe (*pralaya*), which will be followed by a period of inactivity ('Brahma's night') of the same

Lakshmi and Vishnu, resting on the serpent Ananta, awaiting the arrival of a new Brahma's day in this illustration from the end of the 19th century.

length as the corresponding 'day', until a new Universe is created. It is during this period of inactivity that Vishnu, lying on Ananta, the serpent of infinity and eternity, rests, waiting for Brahma to carry out his work of creation once again.

108,470,495,616,000

When Buddha, at the request of Arjuna, explains to him and the other disciples how many basic units there were in a *yojana* (unit of length), he gives the figure of 108,470,495,616,000.

311,040,000,000,000

In *Bhagavad Gita* it is said that the total duration of the life of Brahma is 311,040,000,000,000 human years. In one commentary on the work, it is added that "this impressive longevity, which for us is infinite, does not represent more than a zero in the immensity of eternity".

10^{140}

Asamkhyeya is the Buddhist name for the number 10^{140}. In Sanskrit, the word means 'innumerable'.

18,446,744,073,709,551,615

This 20-digit number can be abbreviated to $2^{64} - 1$. According to the legend of Sessa, it corresponds to the number of grains the Rajah would have to have paid to the person who taught him the game of chess if the teacher asked to be given one grain of wheat (or other cereal of his selection) for the first square, and the quantity was doubled for each of the 64 squares on the board.

An exceptional Indian mathematician: Srinivasa Ramanujan

It is worth devoting a little attention to an exceptional figure from Indian mathematics, Srinivasa Ramanujan (1887–1920), of whom J.E. Littlewood

12,345,654,321 AND THE PYRAMIDAL CONSTRUCTION

This palindromic number appears in an Indian document from the 9th century. Its description is as follows: "Start with the one until reaching six, and then decrease in the same order." We know it refers to the number 12,345,654,321 because it follows the description for the calculation of 111,111 · 111,111. The squares of different numbers made up of 1s give this visually appealing pyramid construction with products that are symmetrical and hence palindromes (read the same from left to right and right to left):

$$
\begin{array}{rccccccccccccccccc}
1^2 = & & & & & & & & & 1 & & & & & & & & \\
11^2 = & & & & & & & & 1 & 2 & 1 & & & & & & & \\
111^2 = & & & & & & & 1 & 2 & 3 & 2 & 1 & & & & & & \\
1{,}111^2 = & & & & & & 1 & 2 & 3 & 4 & 3 & 2 & 1 & & & & & \\
11{,}111^2 = & & & & & 1 & 2 & 3 & 4 & 5 & 4 & 3 & 2 & 1 & & & & \\
111{,}111^2 = & & & & 1 & 2 & 3 & 4 & 5 & 6 & 5 & 4 & 3 & 2 & 1 & & & \\
1{,}111{,}111^2 = & & & 1 & 2 & 3 & 4 & 5 & 6 & 7 & 6 & 5 & 4 & 3 & 2 & 1 & & \\
11{,}111{,}111^2 = & & 1 & 2 & 3 & 4 & 5 & 6 & 7 & 8 & 7 & 6 & 5 & 4 & 3 & 2 & 1 & \\
111{,}111{,}111^2 = & 1 & 2 & 3 & 4 & 5 & 6 & 7 & 8 & 9 & 8 & 7 & 6 & 5 & 4 & 3 & 2 & 1 \\
\end{array}
$$

remarked: "Each of the positive integers was one of his personal friends." Although Ramanujan belonged to the Brahman caste, his parents were poor. He was slow to learn to speak, but soon excelled at school because of his calculation skills. He graduated in mathematics in 1904, but at that time in India, there were no mathematical professions. One anecdote that gives a good idea of the character of Ramanujan is the following: K.S. Srinivasan, a student he had met in Kumbakonam, the city where he lived as a child, said to him one day: "Ramanujan, they all say you are a genius." To which he replied: "What! Me, a genius! Look at my elbow, it will tell you the story." His elbow was dirty, due to the fact that at that time Ramanujan, who was extremely poor, worked on a blackboard, using his elbow as an eraser, which was quicker than using a rag. And he added: "My elbow has become rough and black in making a genius of me!"

Throughout his adult life he noted down equations and symbols in notebooks. It is believed that the notebooks contain between 3,000 and 4,000 theorems, and that almost two thirds of the content was totally new in the world of mathematics,

An Indian stamp in honour of Srinivasa Ramanujan, a mathematical genius who died from tuberculosis at the age of 32.

with the remaining discoveries made independently of earlier mathematicians. Perhaps what is most interesting about the equations in these notebooks is the formal beauty of their representation, a beauty linked to the internal harmony of the mathematical relationships they represent. Note, for example, the symmetry of this equation:

$$1-5\left(\frac{1}{2}\right)^3 +9\left(\frac{1\cdot 3}{2\cdot 4}\right)^3 -13\left(\frac{1\cdot 3\cdot 5}{2\cdot 4\cdot 6}\right)^3 +\ldots = \frac{2}{\pi}.$$

The end of the series, so spectacularly beautiful, is $2/\pi$; and this is to say nothing of the coefficients, 1, 5, 9 and 13, which all differ by 4.

THE SPEED OF RAMANUJAN

On one occasion, a friend asked Ramanujan to find a solution to the following system of equations, which he was unable to solve.

$$\sqrt{x} + y = 7,$$
$$\sqrt{y} + x = 11.$$

Ramanujan immediately replied, "Can you do it yourself?" If you are in any doubt, the solution is $x = 9$ and $y = 4$.

Another one of Ramanujan's beautiful equations is:

$$\cfrac{1}{1+\cfrac{e^{-2\pi}}{1+\cfrac{e^{-4\pi}}{1+...}}} = \left[\sqrt{\left(\frac{5+\sqrt{5}}{2}\right)} - \frac{\sqrt{5}+1}{2}\right] \cdot e^{\frac{2}{5\pi}}.$$

Curiously, what can we discover from this equation? On the right, we can see the golden ratio: $(\sqrt{5} + 1)/2$. This simple discovery is enough to add a certain mystic-mathematical intrigue to its intrinsic beauty.

Finally, an elegant continuous fraction that gives another Ramanujan equation is:

$$\frac{1}{e-1} = \cfrac{1}{1+\cfrac{2}{2+\cfrac{3}{3+\cfrac{4}{4+...}}}}.$$

Ramanujan gave credit for his discoveries to the Hindu goddess Namakkal.

Notable numbers in China

The Chinese were also brilliant in the art of numbers, numbers that have impregnated their mythology and customs from ancient times to the present day.

1

In Chinese numerology, the number 1 is the mystic centre from which all light and multiplicity is derived, and corresponds to the creation hidden behind the diversity of appearances. The number is associated with yang and alludes to man as a being associated with an ascending creation, sometimes expressed by the image of a vertical stone, an erect phallus or a stick. According to the Chinese, everything is derived from one. This is explained by Lao Tse in his work *Tao Te Ching*: "The Tao produced one; one produced two; two produced three; the three produced the ten thousand beings." This is also taught by Master Chuang (Chuang Tse): "The great beginning was Nothingness; there was no Being, nor men. From this was born One. There was One, but there were no corporeal forms. Beings were born from this, and that which would be called Virtue. That which was formless was divided, and from there followed an incessant movement, which is called Destiny, the primitive energy."

A fragment from one of the works of Chuang Tse, a Chinese philosopher from the 4th century BC that includes different aspects of numerology among its teachings.

SEEING 1

Puh Liang states that he reached the Tao in the following way. It took him three days to transcend the world. He then waited three days to transcend all material things. It took nine more days to transcend life in its entirety. Then he turned white and brilliant like the morning and, thanks to this, was able to see 1. Having seen 1, he was able to eliminate the difference between the present and the past, which allowed him to enter into the kingdom of those neither living nor dead.

2

In Chinese mysticism, the primitive duality is reduced to a struggle between yin and yang. Specifically, the number 2 is identified with the sign for yin, the feminine and the earthly. Its feminine quality is projected onto all even numbers; odd numbers, on the other hand, are regarded as masculine.

3

For the Chinese, the number 3 was important because even if there were eight extremes of hardship, there were three guarantees of success. The extremes of hardship were: beauty, beard, height, corpulence, force, elegance, bravery and courage; whoever exceeded others in these characteristics would find themselves in hardship as a result of them. However, if they resort to the three guarantees of success – adapting oneself to the nature of things, behaving like others and showing oneself to be fearful and humble – the hardship could be averted. In other Chinese traditions, the number 3 appears endowed with spectacular powers, defining the most efficient word, the most certain thought and the most sublime idea. It was also the number of unanimity, as shown in the following story. There were once 11 generals whohad to decide

Just like in other cultures, the number 3 and triads are frequent additions to Chinese traditions. This illustration is a painting that shows Confucius introducing Buddha to Lao Tse.

THREE ESSENCES OF ZEN

The study of zen requires three essential things. The first is a great root of faith. The second is a great feeling of amazement. The third is unbreakable perseverance. If one of these elements is missing, the student will be like a tripod missing a leg.

whether to attack or withdraw from a battle. After a long debate, the generals decided to vote. Three decided to attack and eight to withdraw, meaning the final decision was to attack. Why? Because 3 is the number of unanimity.

For Chinese Taoists, there are three higher souls, *houen*, and seven lower souls, *p'o*. After death, the *houen* descend to the subterranean region of the Yellow Springs. There they continue to suffer as souls who miss the body from which they have just separated. The *p'o* souls haunt the tombs and houses where they lived. For Taoists, 'three' also represents the main categories: Heaven, Earth and man.

4

In China, the number 4 is the sign of the Earth, sometimes of the empress, and represents the four forces: strong, weak, light and heavy. From far back in antiquity, the number 4 expressed the world and its dimensions, matter and its components. It also represented totality, the arrangement in four directions. In China, 'four' shows

THE FOUR GODS OF THE SKY

To the left and right of the portal to Buddhist temples stand giant effigies of the four heavenly kings. The largest brandishes a magic sword, Blue Cloud, on whose blade are engraved the signs of the four elements: earth, water, fire, wind. Removing it from its sheath unleashes a black wind that annihilates the bodies of men and turns them to dust. The second holds an umbrella, referred to as the Umbrella of Chaos, a magical artefact that, when opened, darkens the world and, when turned inside out invokes storms and earthquakes. A third plays a lute with four strings; when God plays it, the whole world stops to listen and the enemy camps burn. The fourth holds two whips and has a panther-skin case in which lives a sort of white rat; when let loose, the rat takes the form of an elephant with white wings that feeds off men.

the importance of the quaternary in the configuration of the process of becoming an individual, which, in the final instance is related to the four major functions that orientate inner life: thought, emotion, intuition and feeling.

5

In ancient Chinese writing, the number 5 (*wu*) is represented as a crossing of four elements, to which a line alluding to the centre is added. With the passing of time, 5 came to represent the centre itself. Ancient Chinese cosmology is based on the image of five: there were five colours, five flavours, five sounds, five metals, five internal organs (liver, lungs, heart, kidneys, spleen), five regions, five senses, five elements (water, fire, wood, metal and earth) and so on. The Chinese god of literature and investigation, Zhong-kui, bears a sword with which he frightens away five poisonous animals: the serpent, the centipede, the scorpion, the lizard and the toad.

There were also five canonical books associated with Confucius that made up the *Wu Ching* (literally, 'the five classics'). The set is made up of the following texts: *I Ching* (Book of Changes), *Shu Ching* (Book of History), *Shih Ching* (Book of Songs), *Li Chi* (Book of Ritual) and *Ch'un Ch'iu* (Spring and Autumn Annals).

6

In ancient China, 'six' represented the six breaths: wind, cold, heat, moisture, dryness and inflammation. 6 is also the base of the hexagrams that make it possible to decipher the future in the oracular book *I Ching*.

The hexagram number 61 ('Inner Truth'), one of 64 hexagrams that make up the I Ching, the title of which can be translated as 'Book of Changes'.

The Chinese are accustomed to grouping almost all their reflections on the plastic arts into groups of six. Hence, for example, the six rules of painting: the circulation of chi (vibrations, vital energy) produces vital movement; the brush creates structure; drawing the shape conforms to the object; applying colour corresponds to the nature of the object; composition ensures the elements are in the correct places; and finally, copying attempts to transmit the essence of the methods of the master. These rules were recorded by Hsieh Ho towards the end of the 5th century.

7

For the Chinese, the number 7 has profound mythological roots. There are seven stars visible in Ursa Major and a ceremonial sword with seven stars is used in Taoist rituals, which represents the power to eliminate evil. On the seventh night of the seventh lunar month, a famous traditional Chinese festival takes place to celebrate the romantic story of a young weaver and a boy, celestial shepherds that meet once a year to cross the bridge formed by the Milky Way. In China, the number 7 is also identified with death; hence why there are seven days of mourning. It also embodies the processes of change that give rise to the repetition of cycles, and it represents the hidden essence in every human being. As a symbol, it covers human totality, understood as the union of the following aspects: feminine and masculine, mind and spirit, and once again yin and yang.

Among the Chinese, the seven-tailed fox is an evil genius; saints and sages have 'seven holes' in their hearts; there are seven animal spirits; there are seven fairies with seven colours; and one of the favourite charms of this people is the seven-leafed lotus.

THE SEVEN SAGES OF THE BAMBOO GROVE

At some point around the year 100 BC, an intellectual school of thought referred to as 'pure conversation' developed among neo-Taoists. It became popular among dispossessed intellectuals outside of the administration, and its best-known figures were referred to as the Seven Sages of the Bamboo Grove. They were nonconformists, in a similar way to the Socratic tradition, and held cordial and informal discussions in the open air, lubricated by wine, on spiritual and literary matters. Those who participated in this movement were voluntarily eccentric and anti-establishment.

8

In Taoist mythology, the Eight Immortals play a fundamental role in many artistic works. They arose at a relatively late stage, and until the 15th century, there were no accounts of how they came to be immortal.

In terms of the prose of ancient China, even if there are three classes, there are eight elements that convert it into literature: spirit, principles, vital force, taste, style, rules, tone and colour. The first four represent the essence of literature, whereas the latter are more common elements.

As has been previously mentioned, for the Chinese there were eight extremes of hardship, and there were also eight vices in ancient China: doing what one shouldn't, which was referred to as 'monopolising'; giving counsel to someone who is not interested, or 'practising rhetoric'; speaking to please, or 'flattery'; speaking without distinguishing between true and false, or 'adulation'; taking pleasure in speaking badly of others, or 'gossip'; causing trouble among friends and discord among parents, or 'disturbing'; giving hypocritical praise and indulging in slander to cause harm to another, or 'working with malice'; and being deceitful to people, without distinguishing between good and bad to achieve what one desires, referred to as 'being a gentlemen of fortune'. These eight vices cause outer damage to others and inner damage to oneself.

Finally, for the Chinese, the number 8 represents the eight great manifestations from which the subtle energetic truth of all situations is revealed, as taught by *I Ching*: sky, earth, water, fire, thunder, lake, wind and mountain.

9

For Chinese, 'nine' is both the beginning and the end. It represents the last number of a series and the beginning of a new reality on a higher plane. It corresponds to the image of all that has taken place. It is the number of the determining causes. It represents the culmination of all processes and articulates the image of the three worlds in their inner composition. Similarly, it is related to the capacity to identify oneself with other realities, with understanding, and with spiritual fullness.

10

The ancient Chinese related 'ten' to time, in which it represented change and trans-formation. Just like in the West, the decade has connotations of completeness, which

THE NINE NUMBERS ON THE TORTOISE SHELL

The number 9 is related to the first magic square recorded in history. According to tradition, in the year 2200 BC, a large tortoise, a symbol of eternity, emerged from the River Lo. Its back was covered in different coloured marks, which made up an amazing drawing, as shown in the image.

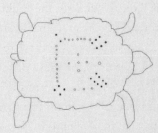

There were nine groups of markings, and substituting each for the number it appeared to represent yielded an arithmetic puzzle. The numbers from 1 to 9 were ordered

Drawing on the shell of the tortoise in the River Lo.

in such a way that, adding their rows, columns or diagonals, always gave the same number: 15. Represented as a traditional magic square, it would have the following layout:

8	1	6
3	5	7
4	9	2

The Great Yu (who was drying out the waters of the flood when the tortoise emerged) took it and studied its strange shell. The drawing inspired his treatise entitled the *Great Plan*, which deals with physics, astrology, fortune-telling, morality, politics and religion. This story appears in one of the four canonical books of ancient China, *Shu Ching (*Book of History*).*

are exemplified in various related myths, such as this example. Ten kings preside over the regions of hell where the dead suffer torture in proportion to their faults. The first king receives the dead and decides if they require punishment or not; if they do, he assigns them to the region to which they must be sent. This role is originally performed by Yen Lo Wang (the Chinese name of the Indian lord of death, Yama). However, he was demoted to the fifth court because of his lenience. The second king covers the region that punishes dishonest messengers, fraudulent administrators and ignorant doctors. The third king is responsible for punishing unfair mandarins, forgers, slanderers and those who pass themselves off as intelligent. The fourth king punishes greedy rich people, thieving traders and those aware of cures that have not shared them. The fifth king torments religious sinners, murderers, hunters and fishermen, and the lustful. The sixth king punishes the sacrilegious. The seventh king punishes those who sell and consume human flesh. The eighth king is responsible for tormenting those who lack filial pity. The ninth king is responsible for punishing arsonists, abortionists, obscene writers and painters and their clients, and also for supervising the city of the accidentally dead, including suicides, for whom there will be no rebirth if they cannot find another accidentally dead to take their place. The tenth king deals with the transmigration that brings the dead to their new existence, through which they can be reborn as gods, human beings on Earth or in hell, good or bad demons, or animals.

12

One consequence of identifying the plastic arts with the number 6 was that the visual tradition became intertwined with its multiples, such as 12. This is why in traditional schools of Chinese painting there are 12 things to be avoided: a full and poorly arranged composition; that the near and far are not clearly distinguished; mountains without *ch'i* (the vital pulse); water without indication of its origin; scenes without inaccessible natural places; paths without indication of their beginning or end; stones and rocks with just a single face; trees with less than four main branches; figures distorted in an unnatural way; poorly placed buildings and pavilions; forgetting the atmospheric effects of mist or clarity; and applying colour without method.

14

In China, there are 14 rules for where and when the lute can be played: upon meeting someone who understands music; upon meeting someone who deserves it; for a retired Taoist; in a large salon; having gone up onto a pavilion of various floors; in a Taoist cloister; sat on a stone; on the top of a mountain; resting in a valley; walking beside a stream; on a boat; resting in a forest in the shade; when the two essences of nature are brilliant and clear; and when there is a full Moon and a fresh breeze.

Likewise, there are 14 rules for where and when it shouldn't be played: when there is wind and thunder or rain; when there is a solar or lunar eclipse; at a legal proceeding; in a market or shop; for a barbarian; for a common person; for a merchant; for a courtesan; while drunk; after making love; when dressed in dirty or eccentric clothing; when suffering from congestion and sweating; without having washed one's hands and brushed one's teeth; and in a noisy place.

Enormous numbers in the Chinese tradition

We saw above how the Indians were great lovers of enormous numbers when it came to defining and interpreting their cosmogony, and part of this love for certain numbers that explain the origin of the world passed to the Chinese. Consider, for example, this passage from *Monkey: Journey to the West*: "In the kingdom of Heaven and Earth, time is divided into periods of one hundred and twenty-nine thousand six hundred years. Each of these is subdivided into twelve epochs lasting ten thousand eight hundred years: Dhzu, Chou, Yin, Mao, Chen, Sz, Wu, Wei, Shen, Yu, Hsü and Hai. [...] At the end of the epoch of Hsü Heaven and Earth lay in a state of total confusion, in which nothingness and everything mixed in a form that is absolutely incomprehensible to us. After five thousand four hundred years of constant darkness, the coming of the epoch of Hai occurred, also known as Chaos, because

AWARE OF EMPTINESS

In *Monkey: Journey to the West* (anonymous, 16th century), we find the following dialogue:

"Let me think," says the venerable old man, looking him firmly in the eyes. "I have given all my other followers a name based on the twelve principles that make up my doctrine and the level they hold within it. You clearly belong to the tenth."

"What principles are those?" asks the monkey king.

"The wide, the large, the wise, the intelligent, the true, the adequate, the natural, the aqueous, the sharp, the aware, the complete and the alert", the venerable old man replies solemnly. "You, as I have just said, belong to the tenth group, or to the aware, expressed using the character *wu*. I have chosen the name of Wu-Kong, that means aware of emptiness. What do you think?"

Illustration from a Chinese edition of Journey to the West, a classic work that combines adventures and spirituality.

THE VALUE OF CALCULATION IN ANCIENT CHINA

The following anecdote dates back to the 9th century. Every so often, two scholars of the same rank, with the same skills and both equally recommended by their reports, aspired to the same position. Not knowing who to promote, the official responsible for the decision asked Yang Sun, who called the candidates to come and see him. He declared:

"The value of minor officials lies in knowing how to calculate quickly; the two candidates should listen to my question; he who gives the answer first will be promoted. A person passing through the forest hears two thieves discussing how to split a number of rolls of cloth they have stolen. He hears them say that if each is given six rolls, five will remain, however if each is given seven, they would lack eight. How many thieves are there and how many rolls of cloth do they have?"

Yang Sun asks the two candidates to make their calculations using sticks on the tiles in the vestibule. After a short while, one of the candidates gives the correct answer (13 thieves, 83 rolls), and is promoted; the officials are dismissed, accepting the decision.

during its dominion there were no human beings and nor were there either of the two spheres by which we are now governed. Another five thousand four hundred years had to pass until reaching the end of such a dark epoch, and the creative forces of life slowly began to act. [...] However, when, after another five thousand four hundred years, spring began to take control of the epoch of Dhzu, the firmament echoed its immobile roots and the light was finally able to form the Sun, the Moon, the stars and the remaining celestial bodies. As such, it is not strange that it is said that heaven began to exist in such a numinous epoch. This was followed by another five thousand four hundred years, during which the firmament solidified forever. [...] However, another five thousand four hundred years would have to pass following the advent of the epoch of Chou, during which certain material shapelessness would condense and thus give rise to the beginning of the five essential elements: water, fire, metal, wood and earth. Another five thousand four hundred years would have to pass before the end of such an extraordinary epoch, at the end of which began the epoch of Yin and everything we know began to rise and be created, as if following the voice of an eternal spring. [...] During the next five thousand four hundred years, beasts, animals and men appeared. In this way, the three forces that govern the fate of nature were established forever: Heaven, the Earth and man, who, has been noted, was born during the miraculous epoch of Yin."

Chapter 5

Ominous Numbers

There are numbers that cause cold sweats. These are numbers that, since the days of yore, have been regarded as ill-fated, numbers believed to attract bad luck or evoke universal suspicion from their link to catastrophic scenarios.

11

Throughout history, 11 has been regarded as an ominous and tragic number... St Augustine thought it was ill-fated, and he has not been the only thinker to hold this belief. In the Kabbalah, the number 11 symbolises maligned occult forces: transition, excess, danger, conflict and martyrdom. Among other peoples and cultures, it is referred to as the 'number of sins' and the 'penitent'. The 11th chapter of *Tao Te Ching* describes a vision of the void.

For early Christian priests, 11 symbolised sin and depravity. The reason for this could be because it was not possible to find any of the qualities of its predecessors in the number, as it exceeds the number of commandments and is less than 12, the number of fortune and perfection. However, certain gnostic schools of thought stand in opposition to this point of view, as 11 disciples were faithful to Jesus Christ, meaning it would come to represent revelation and truth.

The European tradition regards the number 11 as a signal of discord, death and rebirth. Carl Gustav Jung (1875–1961), a Swiss psychologist who formulated the concept of the collective unconscious and developed the idea of archetypes, described the number 11 as a "violent and dying process of transformation".

In the occult and other esoteric fields, the number 11 is the number of conflict and martyrdom. Hence, 11 has an infernal character because it exposes excess (excess over the number of perfection, 10) and also corresponds to the mandorla, (an almond-shaped symbol), the focus point of inversion and the antithesis, because of being 1 plus 1 (like 2, in a certain sense).

Finally, if we had consulted the Chinese oracle *I Ching*, in hexagram 11, *T'ai* (*Peace*), having found a 6 in the first line, the prediction would have been:

> The city all tumbles into the moat.
> Now is not time for an army.
> Give orders to your own people.
> Though this is the correct course reproach cannot be avoided.

13

It is curious to note that depending on geographical location and culture, the same number can be both ill-fated and feared on the one hand, or regarded as a lucky number and the bearer of the most wide-ranging fortunes on the other. This is the case with the number 13. For many people (normally in the West), it is a bad number; for others, it is a lucky number, a most excellent talisman that is often carried engraved in a small medal.

In Graeco-Roman times, people felt a certain aversion towards the number 13 because it came after 12, which was associated with the end. However, 13 was a sacred number for the peoples of the Yucatán region of Mexico.

The number of guests at the Last Supper, represented here according to the vision of Leonardo, together with the role played by Judas, has resulted in an aversion to 13.

THE 14TH GUEST

Néstor Roqueplan (1804–1870), chief editor of *Le Figaro*, was not only a dandy who cultivated an elegance of the most refined sort. He led a busy social life, and was constantly invited to dinners and parties, although there was a secret to his popularity. On his business card, below his name, where the profession of journalist should have appeared, was simply "14th". Hence, he was offering himself to be invited to any meeting or party of 13 other guests.

The ancient Hebrews did not regard 13 as an unlucky number. It appears that this connotation is rooted in the sentencing of Judas after the last supper, as Jesus and his apostles were 12, and the 13th person, Judas, was a traitor. However, this consideration is undermined by the so-called Gospel of Judas, which was used by Gnostics and in which it is insisted that the 12 disciples of Jesus did not understand the role played by Judas as the only one who truly appeared to understand the intimate plans of Jesus. In this light, his treason becomes an act of generosity. Thus Judas is not included in the number of apostles and this is why Jesus called him "the thirteenth". This is why for Gnostics 13 is a positive number.

Some people in the West might prefer to go hungry than dine at a table with 13 guests. This is best illustrated by the following anecdote: Victor Hugo, the famous French writer, having been invited to a gala dinner realised there were 13 places at the table. Instead of taking his seat at the table, he declared to those who were present: "Dear friends, there is a superstitious person present in our midst who will not take their place at the table so long as the number of guests remains 13." One of the guests replied, "Who is this imbecile?" To which Victor Hugo replied, "I am that imbecile." It is also said that Queen Elizabeth II scrutinises the plans for her flights, meetings and other plans when travelling to ensure these do not include the number 13.

The number 13 played an important role in the life of the writer James Joyce. It is no coincidence that in the portrait caricature drawn by Abin of the Irish writer in the shape of a question mark, Joyce is wearing a black bowler hat. This is a symbol of mourning for the recent death of his father, it is covered in spider cobwebs and the number 13 appears on it. The number 13 is also the number of death attributed by Bloom to the mysterious man in the macintosh. It was an ambivalent number for Joyce, as he believed it sometimes brought luck. However, for him, it meant death: his mother had died on the 13th and Joyce himself would also die on the 13th.

THE FEAR OF 13 IN LITERATURE

Joaquim Maria Machado de Assis' *Memorias Póstumas de Blas Cubas* includes the following fragment.

> "She told me her husband would reject the appointment for one reason, which he only shared with her, asking her to keep it secret: not to tell anyone else."
>
> "It's naive", he had said, "it's ridiculous; but in short, it is a powerful reason for me."
> And he told her that the decree would be dated the 13th, and that this number evoked gloomy memories for him. His father had died on the 13th, 13 days after a meal with 13 guests. The house in which he had died was also number 13. It was a fateful figure. He couldn't say this to the minister; he would say he had private reasons for not accepting.
> I was – as the reader must be – slightly amazed at this sacrifice for a number. However, as Lobo Neves was so ambitious, the sacrifice must have been genuine...

In Hindu mythology, and according to Roberto Calasso, the number also has an ominous character. The Prajapati numbers were 13, 17 and 34. The first numbers were the numbers of the excess that exceeded a whole (12, 16) in which Prajapati took refuge. Everyone takes care to avoid these numbers, because they do not wish to come up against Prajapati (the Lord of Creatures).

Finally, we shall note some practical consequences of this fear of the number 13. The airlines Iberia and Alitalia do not have a row number 13 in the seating plans for any of their aircraft (at least up until a few years ago); Renault has designed the models of its cars from the number 3 to 21, omitting model 13. In many Western cities, there is no door number 13 in streets; similarly, 13 is forbidden in many hotels, which exclude it from their room numbers. In the tarot pack, card 13 corresponds to 'death'.

17

The Pythagoreans detested 17 because it stood between 16, which is a square, and 18, which is double a square. Moreover, these two numbers are the only numbers that represent areas for which the perimeters (of the corresponding rectangles) are equal to their respective areas.

Throughout the world, the number 17 arouses a form of fear and is associated with many misfortunes, being regarded by many people as just as ill-fated as 13. In Italy, 17 is regarded as so ill-fated that it is avoided in raffles. To corroborate this reputation of misfortune, it is said that during a car race that took place in 1926, the driver Giulio Masetti died just as he was on the 17th kilometre, driving a car whose number was 171. Another driver, Moll, in another race, died on the 17th corner, which coincidentally was located at the 17th kilometre. Such is the apprehension aroused by the number among Italians, that the French car manufacturer Renault changed the name of its R17 car to R177 in order to be able to sell it on the Italian market. When Italians come up against the Roman numeral XVII, they change it to an anagram, VIXI, which means 'I lived' in Latin.

However, 17 is not only regarded as ill-fated in the West. In Hindu mythology, as we saw for 13, the number 17 also has an ominous character, as the Prajapati numbers were 13, 17 and 34.

666

Without a shadow of doubt, 666 takes first place in the league of ominous numbers, in this case even apocalyptic. It comes from an apocalypse described in the *Revelation of St John*. The number, identified in the Bible with the Beast or Antichrist, has been the preferred choice of prophets and numerologists throughout the course of time. For the Kabbalah, the number 666 corresponds to the alphabetic transcription of Nero Caesar. However, it is not only they that have sought a personal meaning for the famous number. In the 16th century, a Catholic author wrote a book in which he proved that Martin Luther was the Antichrist, as according to the Latin spelling, the value of his name was 666. This Catholic apologist (Petrus Bungus, *Numerorum Mysteria*), first tried his calculation with the name Martin Luther, but when this did not give him the value he was seeking, he changed the name Luther to Lutera, its Latin version. With this small change, he applied the following numeric table (note that I and J were the same letters, as were U and V; there was no W):

A	1	K	10	T	100
B	2	L	20	U or V	200
C	3	M	30	X	300
D	4	N	40	Y	400
E	5	O	50	Z	500
F	6	P	60		
G	7	Q	70		
H	8	R	80		
I or J	9	S	90		

This gave Bungus the result he required:

M	30	L	20
A	1	U	200
R	80	T	100
T	100	E	5
I	9	R	80
N	40	A	1

TOTAL = 260 + 406 = 666.

The reply from the reformist camp was not long in coming. Using the same technique, a Protestant published a proof that the words on the Papal tiara ('Vicar of the Son of God') also gave 666 when adding the Roman numerals included in the Latin version of the phrase. Hence:

VICARIVS FILII DEI $\quad$ (5 + 1 + 100 + 1 + 5 + 1 + 50 + 1 + 1 + 500 + 1 = 666).

In 1554, another anti-Papist, Michael Stifel, or Stifelius (1487–1567), published a new edition of a book on algebra that was one of the first in which the signs '+' and '−' were used. The edition included Stifelius' own calculations of the number of the Beast. Fixing his sights on Pope Leo X, he proposed translating the name into numbers using its Latin form: Leo Decimus. Stifelius tried applying the same treatment to the Pope's name as Bungus had done with Martin Luther, and discovered that the numbers only added up to 416 (leaving 250 to reach 666). As is often the case with numerologists, he began to use false numbers.

Stifelius broke from Bungus' system and selected just the letters L, D, C, I, M and V from the Pope's name (note U = V). These were the letters that also represented Roman numerals. He then removed the M, arguing that it meant *misterium* (mystery) and should be ruled out on this ground. Finally, he added an X, which represented 10 in Leo X. Arranging the Roman numerals in descending order, Stifelius obtained DCLXVI (500 + 100 + 50 + 10 + 5 + 1), or 666. Hence, using the appropriate manipulation, he managed to show that the name Leo X is equivalent to the Beast from the Apocalypse.

Clearly, this unscientific method of numerological manipulation also allows complete freedom of interpretation. For a US Democrat, it would not have been

*Cover of the book
in which Stifelius
predicted the date of the
Apocalypse, based on his
mathematical calculations.
The predicted date was 19
October 1533.*

difficult to discover that the name Ronald Wilson Reagan is made up of three six-lettered words, giving a peculiar 666. Following this method, and applying the numeric representation of the Hebrew alphabet, it is perhaps significant that the name Saddam has the following value: *samech* (60) + *aleph* (1) + *daled* (4) + *aleph* (1) + *mem* (600) = 666.

The modern craze for seeking the value 666 in the names of political enemies dates back, according to my sources, to Leo Tolstoy's novel *War and Peace*, in which the technique is used. In chapter 19 of the third book of the first part, we read: 'One of his brother Masons had revealed to Pierre the following prophecy concerning Napoleon, drawn from the *Revelation of St. John*. In chapter 13, verse 18, of the Apocalypse, it is said: 'Here is wisdom. Let him that hath understanding count the number of the beast: For it is the number of a man; and his number is Six hundred threescore and six.' And in the fifth verse of the same chapter: 'And there was given unto him a mouth speaking great things and blasphemies; and power was given unto him to continue forty and two months.' The French alphabet, written out with the same numerical values as the Hebrew, in which the first nine letters denote units and the others tens, will be as follows:'

1	2	3	4	5	6	7	8	9	10	20	30	40	50	60	70	80	90	100	110	120	130	140	150	160
a	b	c	d	e	f	g	h	i	k	l	m	n	o	p	q	r	s	t	u	v	w	x	y	z

Apparently the politician William Gladstone (1809–1898) had so many enemies that one of them even used numerology in an attempt to discredit him. The image shows the British politician making use of the word in a parliamentary debate in 1886, as shown in the Illustrated London News.

"Writing the words 'L'Empereur Napoleon' in numbers, it appears that the sum of them is 666, and that Napoleon was therefore the beast foretold in the Apocalypse. Moreover, by applying the same system to the words 'quarante-deux', which was the term ascribed to the Beast that 'spoke great things and blasphemies', the same number 666 was obtained; from which it followed that the limit fixed for Napoleon's power had come in the year 1812 when the French emperor was 42."

Sticking with politicians and the number of the beast, an enemy of William Gladstone, prime minister of the United Kingdom, wrote GLADSTONE in Greek, added the numbers together and obtained 666. The number has also been identified with HITLER, even though the numbers assigned to the letters follow the pattern: A = 100, B = 101, C = 102... This gives:

H	107
I	108
T	119
L	111
E	104
R	117
	666

---

666 ACCUSES BILL GATES

The most modern – and peculiar – application of the numerology of the beast is against the Microsoft tycoon Bill Gates. The American magazine *Harper* featured the numeric conversion of Gates' name, which is William Henry Gates III in full (note the III, a typical trick used by numerologists to achieve their goals). The magazine did not use a conventional language, but the ASCII values of the letters. Hence, in ASCII, Bill Gates 3 is equivalent to: 66 + 73 + 76 + 76 + 71 + 65 + 84 + 69 + 83 + 3 = 666.

This is the first record of the ASCII alphabet (a = 64, b = 65..., z = 89) being used for gematria. Adding 1 to Windows 95 also gives 666.

However, 666 appears earlier in the Bible without the ominous characterisation it received from St John. In Kings (10:14), it is said that the number corresponds to the number of golden talents received by Solomon in a year, and in Ezra (2:13), it is said that 666 is the number of children of Adoniquam, whose name means 'Lord of Enemies'. Spookily, however, Revelation is in the 66th book of the Bible and 666 is mentioned in verse 18, in other words 6 + 6 + 6.

However, not everyone in the world is scared of the number. Some people even like it. In 1988, the owner of number 666 North Lake Shore Drive in Chicago changed the number to 668. However, the tenants protested because they liked the old number; in 1994, the New Mexico Department of Transportation refused to change the name of the US Highway 666, whose name dated back to 1926. In this way, the government of New Mexico fought against superstition.

Other 666-related curiosities

For the Eastern Orthodox Church, 666 is regarded as symbolic as in Greek numbers, 666 alludes to Christ.

The number was used as a pseudonym by Aleister Crowley, an English ceremonial magician and follower of the occult, who named himself the Beast referred to in the Revelation.

The première of the 2006 remake of the horror movie *The Omen* was held on 06/06/06 (6 June 2006) at 06:06:06.

As we have already mentioned, the full name of President Ronald Wilson Reagan contains six letters in each of its three components, which led certain numerologists, such as Gatry D. Blevins, to believe Reagan was the Antichrist. The curious thing about this story is that when former president Reagan moved to California, he requested his house number be changed from 666 (its original number) to 668. It would appear he was followed by the number.

The number 666 was the original name of the Macintosh computer virus *SevenDust* discovered in 1998.

Six Sixty Six is the title of a song by the pioneer of Christian rock, Larry Nonnan. A version of the song was recorded by Frank Black and the Catholics.

The first Apple computer, the *Apple 1*, was launched at a price of $666.66.

Aversion to the number 666 is called hexakosioihexekontahexaphobia or triplehexaphobia.

Another demonic property of this ill-fated number is that the numbers of a roulette wheel add up to 666.

A city in the state of Louisiana in the United States changed its telephone prefix (666) to prevent it being associated with the devil.

Finally, note that from a purely Pythagorean point of view, the ratio between the lunar number 1,080, and the solar number 666, is an amazing approximation to the golden ratio, phi $(\Phi) = (\sqrt{5}+1)/2 = 1.618$. And if it is 6s we are talking about, and beasts, remember that the Pythagorean triangle with sides 693, 1,924 and 2,045, has an area of 666,666, two 'beasts' in a row.

666, a most playful arithmetic number

In addition to being heavily used in less-than-cheerful prophecies and the predictions of cataclysms, 666 is also commonly used in arithmetic. Here are some of the curious algebraic properties of this dark prince of numbers.

---

666 IN CHEMISTRY

The medicinal product Salvarsan (an amphetamine, referred to as a 'magic bullet' by its inventor Paul Ehrlich) is a preparation of organic arsenic used to treat syphilis and relapsing fever. It was nicknamed 606 by its inventor because, he claimed, it was the result of 606 experiments. This name was subsequently distorted to 666. The number 666 is also used to refer to a powerful insecticide: hexachlorocyclohexane, whose formula is $C_6H_6Cl_6$.

ARITHMETIC PUZZLES INVOLVING THE NUMBER OF THE BEAST

Introduce three signs into the sequence 123456789 (the numbers from 1 to 9 in ascending order) so they add up to 666.

Solution: $123 + 456 + 78 + 9 = 666$. If we allow the use of negative numbers (except at the start of the series), the sequence would be: $1234 - 567 + 8 - 9 = 666$. If we were set the challenge of introducing four signs (of any sign) into the same series of numbers, the answer would be: $9 + 87 + 6 + 543 + 21 = 666$.

Numeric Relationships

666 is the sum of its digits plus the cubes of its digits: $666 = 6 + 6 + 6 + 6^3 + 6^3 + 6^3$ (only six numbers exist with this property).

It is a divisor of $123,456,789 + 987,654,321$ (note that these numbers are the union of all the digits from 1 to 9 and 9 to 1).

It can be represented as a palindromic summation of cubes: $666 = 1^3 + 2^3 + 3^3 + 4^3 + 5^3 + 6^3 + 5^3 + 4^3 + 3^3 + 2^3 + 1^3$.

Pythagorean and triangular numeric relationships

It is the 36th triangular number: $T(6 \cdot 6) = 666 = 1 + 2 + 3 + 4 \ldots + 34 + 35 + 36$ (and $36 = 6 \cdot 6$). It is the smallest triangular number of the form $a^2 + b^2$, where $a + b$ is also triangular, e.g. $T(6 \cdot 6) = 666 = T(5)^2 + T(6)^2 = 15^2 + + 21^2$, where 15 and 21 are consecutive triangular numbers.

The triplet (216, 630, 666) is a Pythagorean triplet (the sum of the squares of the first two = the square of the third): $216^2 + 630^2 = 666^2$.

Relationships with important constants

It is the sum of the first 144 digits of π, where $144 = (6 + 6) \cdot (6 + 6)$.

Relationships with other numbering systems

In Roman numerals, 666 is written as DCLXVI, the first six Roman numerals in descending order.

Relationships with prime numbers

It is the sum of two consecutive prime palindromes: $666 = 313 + 353$. It is the sum of the squares of the first seven prime numbers: $666 = 2^2 + 3^2 + 5^2 + + 7^2 + 11^2 + 13^2 + 17^2$.

Other properties

It is a 'repdigit' number (a number with all its digits the same). However, as a repdigit it has a property that is not shared with numbers of the same class: it is the largest triangular repdigit.

It is a Smith number: $666 = 2 \cdot 3 \cdot 3 \cdot 37$ and $6 + 6 + 6 = 2 + 3 + 3 + 3 + 7$.

Finally, the number 666 has its own magic square, a magic square of the sixth order $(6 \cdot 6)$ and whose constant is 666.

The square is as follows:

3	107	5	131	109	311	666
7	331	193	11	83	41	666
103	53	71	89	151	199	666
113	61	97	197	167	31	666
367	13	173	59	17	37	666
73	101	127	179	139	47	666
666	666	666	666	666	666	

A special case: 23, the number of conspiracy

"Two-digit numbers express
a relationship between them, from left to right.
For example, 23 = 2 (conflict) 3 (solved)."
Conspiracy axiom

The number 23 is a rising star in modern symbology and the darling of conspiracy theorists. For example: 2 plus 3 gives 5, the number with which the devil can be invoked. Dividing 2 by 3 gives 0.666, the number of the Beast. The dates of the assassinations of John F. Kennedy and Lee Harvey Oswald, the 22nd and 24th of November, respectively, have a significant gap: 23. Almost all the great anarchists have died on the 23rd day of the month: Sacco and Vanzetti on 23 August, Bonny and Clyde on 23 May, Dutch on 23 October and Vince Cool was 23 years old when he was shot in street number

23; although John Dillinger died on 22 of July, it is also the case that 23 others died in Chicago that same night, all as a result of a heatwave. According to Dr Lightfoot, who was Vice Chancellor of Cambridge University, the world began on 23 October 4004 BC. The Hungarian revolution began on 23 October and Harpo Marx was born on 23 November. According to Seutonius, Caesar was stabbed exactly 23 times by Brutus and his assassins. Finally, recall that Bloomsday, the day that commemorates the day on which the events of James Joyce's *Ulysses* takes place, is in the year 1904, and 19 + 04 gives 23.

Since the publication of the *Illuminatus Trilogy* by Robert Anton Wilson, which relates the number 23 to paranormal phenomena and conspiracy theories, many people (mainly in the United States it must be said) have dedicated themselves to following 23 through space and time, and this number, generous and prolific, has appeared in almost any circumstance. In addition to the records of the preceding paragraph, there are also many other examples in which, through this number, one can feel the hand of conspiracy:

The chat domains of AOL (America OnLine, once the world's largest Internet service provider) limit the number of users that can be connected at a given moment in time to 23.

In the film *Airport*, the madman who carries the bomb is in seat number 23.

In the air disaster *TWA 800*, which was attributed to a conspiracy, there were 230 deaths.

The letter W is the 23rd in the English alphabet and has two points facing downwards and three facing upwards.

The first lunar landing of Apollo took place at 23.63° east, and the second at 23.42° west.

Outer space is also a realm for numerology.
The Apollo 11 *mission, which took the first men to the Moon,*
was apparently marked by the number 23.

Area 51, the name by which a secret government base is known (a facility that is allegedly shared by the CIA and extra-terrestrials, according to those who believe in such things), can be broken down into $23 + 23 + (2 + 3) = 51$.

William Wallace, a Scottish noble who led the uprising against English occupation was executed under accusations of treason on 23 August 1305.

Both the series *Star Trek* and *Babylon Five* were set in the 23rd century.

At the moment of conception, father and mother each contribute 23 chromosomes.

According to a fashionable Mayan prophecy, the world will end on 23 December 2012. Note that 2012 can be broken down into: $(20 + 1 + 2 = 23)$.

The impeachment of President Nixon was based on article 2, section 3 of the United States Constitution.

The first prime number with both digits prime is 23.

The Number 23 is the title of the film directed by Joel Schumacher, in which Jim Carrey is the lead actor. The story is based on Walter Sparrow and his wife Agatha. Theirs is normal marriage, which after reading a mysterious book entitled *The Number 23*, becomes engulfed in a series of strange events in which the fictional events of the book begin to mix with reality, giving rise to a strange combination of parallel worlds, where paranoia, fear, fiction and crime are the common denominator in both Universes. The names of the actor, Jim Carrey, and the director, Joel Schumacher, add up to a total of 23 letters (curiously, Jim Carrey's production company is called JC23).

There were 23 Grand Masters of the Knights Templar.

The *Titanic* sunk on the morning of 15 April 1912 and $(1 + 5 + 4 + 1 + 9 + 1 + 2 = 23)$.

Two of the best basketball players in history were Michael Jordan (jersey number 23) and Magic Johnson (jersey 32)

The 'Immortal Game' of chess played between Anderssen and Kieseritzky lasted only 23 moves.

'Mole Day', 23 October, is celebrated by chemists from 6:02 in the morning until 6:02 in the evening in honour of the Avogadro number, which is approximately $6.023 \cdot 10^{23}$.

The earthquake that occurred in Tokyo in 1923 caused Japan's gross national product to fall by a third.

The writer Rynosuke Akutagawa, in his book *Rashomon*, narrates the life of a patient in a lunatic asylum under the codename NQ 23.

On Friday 23 July, in the luxurious Belgioioso Palace in Milan, Raul Gardini shot himself in the right temple with a PPK (initials of the German pistol used by

THE NUMBER 23 AND THE BOOK OF THE HIDDEN

The chapter of the *Zohar* entitled *The Book of the Hidden*, states there are "twenty-three invisible letters and twenty-three visible ones. One Yod is hidden; one Yod is visible. The visible and the invisible are balanced on the Scale." Weave and warp link the invisible and the visible. Some adherents to the Kabbalah talk of a twenty-third letter, the missing letter, that which is hidden in the blank spaces, in the spaces of reflection between the other letters.

Cover of the 1558 Mantua edition of the Zohar.

criminal police and James Bond), calibre 7.65. Raul Gardini was the head of the Ferruzzi-Montedison Group. The bed on which he was found lying had two of the day's newspapers open at pages reporting the statements of Giuseppe Garofano, nicknamed 'El Cardenal', recently extradited from Geneva, a distinguished member of Opus Dei and whose confession left Gardini exposed to prosecution. Was the date chosen because of its significance as part of a conspiracy, or was it just chance, a coincidence?

Many of us might think that these are just simple coincidences, however... What if they were something more? What is true, is at the time I stopped writing this text, my watch read 18:05. Can you guess what the sum of 18 and 5 is? Of course... 23.

Not even the gods or demi-gods can free themselves from suffering the persecutions of this number of conspiracy. According to tradition, the daughters of Mara approached Buddha from the bushes, sweet and sorrowful: "We want to worship your feet, oh happy being", they said. Buddha did not stop. Then the girls followed him closer, even brushing up against him. "The desire of men takes on many different forms..." they repeated. Buddha showed no sign of having heard them. The girls stopped to agree another strategy. "We shall transform ourselves. We shall turn ourselves into hundreds of girls aged 15 or 16", said Tanha. Arati agreed. Now Buddha walked surrounded by an entourage of girls who engaged in the 23

THE NUMBER 23 AND COINCIDENCES

The number 23 also appears in synchronicities, which is the name given by Carl G. Jung to a certain type of non-causal coincidence. The best known of these involves the novelist William Burroughs. Burroughs states that when he lived in Tangier in 1958 (its digits add up to 23), he had a conversation with a certain Captain Clark, who mentioned to him that he had been sailing the strait for 23 years without any mishaps. That same day Captain Clark suffered his first serious accident. That same afternoon, as he was talking about the event, Burroughs heard a news bulletin on the radio about an air accident in Florida. The flight number was 23 and the pilot was a certain Captain Clark.

Another curious 'coincidence' involving 23 is as follows. After Arthur Koestler had published his *Roots of Coincidence*, the academic Hans Zeisel, at the University of Chicago, wrote to Koestler explaining to him how he was followed everywhere by a chain of instances of the number 23. In Vienna, his home city, he lived in the street Rossaurerlaend 23. His legal practice was at Gonzagagasse 23 and his mother lived at Alserstrasse 23. On one occasion, Zeisel's mother took a copy of the novel entitled *Die Liebe der Jeanne Ney*, in which a character wins a fortune at roulette betting on 23 in Monte Carlo. Zeisel's mother attempted to repeat the luck of the character from the novel and bets on 23 in the casino. The number 23 came up on her second attempt.

gestures of female seduction. They all repeated: "We want to worship your feet, oh happy being." The forest was invaded by a delicate chatter. Buddha kept walking. Shortly after, the girls, tired of their unfruitful attempts, gave up. Finally, Buddha sat down below a tree.

Thus ends this exploration of the Universe of numbers. It has been divided into six chapters, including the preface, and 6, as we have noted, is a perfect number. I can only hope that this attribute has rubbed off on this book, albeit to the slightest extent.

Bibliography

COHEN, I.B., *The Triumph of Numbers. How Counting Changed Modern Life*, New York, W.W. Norton & Co., 2006.

GARDNER, M., *The Colossal Book of Mathematics: Classic Puzzles, Paradoxes and Problems*, New York, W.W. Norton & Co., 2001.

IFRAH, G., *The Universal History of Numbers*, Hoboken, Wiley, 2000.

MCLEISH, J., *The Story of Numbers. How Mathematics Has Shaped Civilisations*, New York, Random House, 1994.

—, *The Penguin Dictionary of Mathematics*, edited by David Nelson, London, Penguin, 2008.

WELLS, D., *The Penguin Dictionary of Curious and Interesting Numbers*, London, Penguin, 1997.

Index